Translation as Text

Translation Studies

TRANSLATION STUDIES
Albrecht Neubert, Gert Jäger, and Gregory M. Shreve, Editors

1 *Translation as Text*
Albrecht Neubert and Gregory M. Shreve

Translation Studies is the successor of the German language series *Übersetzungswissenschaftliche Beiträge*, published since 1978 in Leipzig, Germany.

Translation as Text

Albrecht Neubert

&

Gregory M. Shreve

The Kent State University Press
KENT, OHIO, AND LONDON, ENGLAND

© 1992 by The Kent State University Press, Kent, Ohio 44242
ALL RIGHTS RESERVED
Library of Congress Catalog Card Number 92-7731
ISBN 0-87338-469-5
ISBN 978-0-87338-695-1 (pbk.)
Manufactured in the United States of America.

First paperback edition, 2000.

Library of Congress Cataloging-in-Publication Data
Neubert, Albrecht.
Translation as text / Albrecht Neubert and Gregory M. Shreve.
p. cm.—(Translation studies ; 1)
Includes bibliographical references and index.
ISBN 0-87338-469-5 (alk. paper) ∞
ISBN 0-87338-695-7 (pbk.)
1. Translating and interpreting. 2. Discourse analysis.
I. Shreve, Gregory M., 1950– . II. Title. III. Series.
P306.N45   1992
418'.02—dc20   92-7731

British Library Cataloging-in-Publication data are available.

Contents

Preface *vii*

1 **TRANSLATION, TEXT, TRANSLATION STUDIES**

Translation and Paradox *1*
Translation(s) and Text *4*
Unity and Difference in Translation Studies *7*
Models of Translation *12*
The Critical Model *16*
The Practical Model *18*
The Linguistic Model *19*
The Text-linguistic Model *22*
The Sociocultural Model *25*
The Computational Model *26*
The Psycholinguistic Model *29*
Translation Theory: A Prologue *32*

2 **TRANSLATION: KNOWLEDGE AND PROCESS**

Language as System and Language in Use *36*
Translations as Interaction Structures *40*
Translation as Process *43*
Knowledge and Mutual Knowledge *53*
Copresence *56*
Frames *59*
Scenarios, Schemas, Plans, Scripts *65*

3 **TEXTUALITY**

Textuality and "Textness" *69*
Intentionality *70*

Acceptability 73
Situationality 84
Informativity 88
Coherence 93
Cohesion 102
Intertextuality 117

4 TRANSLATION AS RESULT

Translation Evolution 124
Text Types 125
Prototypes 130
Textual Meaning 135
Macrostructures and Macrorules 137
Communicative Value 140
Textual and Communicative Equivalence 142
Text and Translation Theory: An Epilogue 146

Notes 149

References 159

Index 166

Preface

Translation as Text is the direct successor of the volume *Text and Translation*, published as *Übersetzungswissenschaftliche Beiträge* 8 in 1985. Positive response to the original monograph and its successful use as a reference in advanced translation classes in Germany and other countries encouraged us to extensively revise the volume and add new material. We have attempted to clarify the theoretical position and methodological assumptions that were implicit in the earlier version. A new first chapter places the volume in the context of the variety of modern approaches to translation. The monograph describes translation studies as the empirical study of the relationships among translator, the process of translation, and the text.

Translation studies has abandoned its single-minded concern with strictly linguistic issues. It has been invigorated by new ideas from other disciplines. Translation scholars no longer hesitate to adopt new ideas from information science, cognitive science, and psychology. Scholars in these other disciplines have also taken up issues relevant to the study of translation. Translation provides them with unique opportunities to study the dynamics of text production and text comprehension. This interdisciplinary give-and-take has resulted in new research directions. Translation has become an important area of study in its own right.[1]

When translation studies first began to mature as a modern academic discipline, it was viewed as a minor sub-discipline of traditional philology and linguistics. During the fifties, the sixties, and the seventies, academic studies in translation and interpreting had to struggle for legitimacy in traditional philological curricula. Students of translation found it difficult to convince other scholars that the process of translation was a subject worthy of study. The goal of translation studies was to establish that translation was more than a complex form of reading languages or a mechanical skill natural to bilinguals.

The development of translation studies over the last two decades has been characterized by a decline in the influence of linguistics and a movement to give translation research an interdisciplinary focus. Linguistics is now just one of many disciplines which contribute to our understanding of translation. As a result of the emergence of translation as an interdiscipline, new research patterns have emerged which redefine the character of translation studies.[2]

Certainly, translation is still a subject of interest in linguistics. Similarly, linguistics is still a central issue in translation studies. Translation, however, is no longer wholly included in linguistics. Translation studies has emerged to pursue its own connections with other disciplines. The resulting hybrid vigor has led to the growth of a number of competing models of translation. Translation scholars and professional translators focus on different aspects of translation. Each student of translation selects certain parts of the common object of study for attention. The perspectives that result from this selective attention have created different models of translation. The development of multiple understandings of a common phenomenon is characteristic of an emerging and evolving discipline.[3] *Translation as Text* is a contribution to the ongoing evolution of translation studies.

The volume assumes a textual perspective on translation. The textual perspective, because it makes the text the primary object of research, has the potential to act as a unifying concept in the discipline. This perspective respects more narrowly focused perspectives on translation by providing a framework for understanding how various translation processes and results may be reconciled in the concept of translation as text. The text, and the features which give it textuality, are proposed as an integrating concept for the interdiscipline of translation. The textual perspective reminds us that the daily practice of translation is text-centered. The translator takes knowledge from texts and puts knowledge into texts. That is why no concept should be more natural for the student of translation than the concept of textuality.

Practical results should emerge from an improved theoretical understanding of translation. A more effective and coherent study of translation should have real benefits for the teaching of translation, the practice of translation, and even the design of computer-assisted translation systems. We cannot hope to teach effectively, practice translation more competently, or design useful software more efficiently without a comprehensive descriptive understanding of translation as an empirical phenomenon. The observable facts of translation are manifested in texts. Translation scholars, translation teachers, and translators need a common frame of reference. If, by providing this common frame of reference, *Translation as Text* succeeds in establishing the basis for integrating the different perspectives of scholars, readers, critics, teachers, and translators, it would perform a useful service. It is our firm conviction that further progress in translation studies depends on the willingness of scholars to work together. Instead of arguing from unique and insular positions, they should strive for a more global understanding of translation as text.

We would like to express our appreciation for the encouragement of our colleagues in the Department of Theoretical and Applied Linguistics at the University of Leipzig and in the Institute for Applied Linguistics at Kent State University. We are also grateful to Dr. Bob Clawson, Dr. Mark Rubin, Dr. Rudolph Buttlar, Dr. Thomas Moore, and Dr. Michael Schwartz for having the wisdom to encourage the international exchange that has led to the publication of this volume and the *Translation Studies* series. A heartfelt thank you from one author to Dean Thom Lamb for first suggesting that a Kent State linguist visit his colleagues in Leipzig. We especially appreciate the support of the members of the "Leipzig Group," Dr. Klaus Gommlich, Dr. Christina Schäffner, and Dr. Willi Scherf. A special acknowledgement goes to our English language copy editors, Dr. Emil Sattler and Mrs. Joan Shreve, for their extensive work on the manuscript.

Translation as Text

ONE

Translation, Text, Translation Studies

TRANSLATION AND PARADOX

Translation has been an important part of cultural interaction for many centuries. Even with this long history, translation is a paradox. It is natural because we have always done it. Sometimes it seems quite unnatural, especially when we read bad translations. Translation is necessary, but doing it correctly sometimes seems impossible. There have always been social and economic conditions which create a demand for translation. Because of that demand, translators do their work and do it effectively, despite the differences of culture and language that separate the peoples of the world. Translation has evolved quite naturally over the course of human history. It has evolved as a unique answer to a basic human need for intercultural communication. The term *language mediation,* the collective name for translation and interpreting, underscores this crucial role. Still, translation is basically an unnatural act. The whole premise of translation seems problematic. How can we possibly use a foreign language to convey messages originally expressed in another language? The potential for distortion and loss of meaning is immense. A source text is embedded in a complex linguistic, textual, and cultural context. Its meaning, communicative intent, and interpretive effect draw upon its natural relationships in that environment. It is a daunting task to pull a text from its natural surroundings and recreate it in an alien linguistic and cultural setting. The text belongs to a dynamic cultural and linguistic ecology. The translator uproots it in a valiant attempt to transplant its fragile meaning. Translation certainly seems unnatural. Many translations sound unnatural as well. This is vivid testimony to the inherent difficulties of the process.

As unnatural as translation may seem, it is a necessary transgression. Our complex global civilization demands it. The need for translation is exploding with the growth of international communication. It seems proper, recognizing the need for greater human communication, to try to see translation as the most natural of endeavors. Looking at translation as a natural act emphasizes the similarities of disparate languages and cultures. The alternate view emphasizes their differences. Some of those who focus on cultural difference are convinced that there are fewer human universals than we might care to admit. They suggest that translation is impossible. These critics claim that translators actually do violence to texts when they rip them from their natural settings. Venuti expresses an opinion like this when he says that translation is akin to terrorism (Venuti 1991). He claims that "the power of translation" is its ability "to (re)constitute and cheapen foreign texts, to trivialize and exclude foreign cultures, and thus potentially to figure in racial discrimination and ethnic violence, international political confrontations, terrorism, and war." Venuti proposes *resistive translation* as a solution. This kind of translation highlights the "foreignness" of the source text by embedding stylistic or other discontinuities in the target text.

From this highly critical perspective, translation seems at odds with natural monolingual discourse. It is burdened with a perennial bias. Venuti's condemning definition of translation follows inexorably: "translation is the forcible replacement of the linguistic and cultural difference of the foreign text with a text that will be intelligible to the target language reader" (Venuti 1991). This view quite appropriately stresses the potential destructiveness of translation. Translation always involves loss. Every experienced translator knows and accepts this. Like all of nature, translation is entropic; it is a linguistic example of the second law of thermodynamics. There is always semantic loss from the source text at this convergence of cultural systems. Translation destroys the original linguistic form of the source text as well. As a result, the target community absorbs the foreign text and obliterates its differences. Venuti's criticism is source-centered; he looks at what is lost. If there is loss, there may be gain. This is also a paradox of translation.

The target audience may be enriched instead of impoverished. Even if the translation cannot transfer everything in the source text, it still brings benefit to the target culture. If there were nothing of value, readers in the target culture would not demand translations. Even if we concede that preserving everything in the source text is impossible, the translation pessimist must still agree that something is transferred in the translation. Not all foreign values and meanings must disappear during the transfer. To say that everything of value in the foreign text is bound to its linguistic form is too extreme. It implies that the linguistic and textual systems of the target language are hostile to the values of the foreign text. It implies that information content cannot be separated from linguistic and textual form.

Translation has always been a unique source of knowledge and wisdom for mankind. Translation arises from a deep-seated need to understand and come to terms with otherness. We want to know what other people know and feel what other people feel. Of course, there is always the possibility that our view of other cultures will be distorted by translation. Translation may be turned to the service of political and ideological agendas. The capacity of translation for violence, however, is no greater than its capacity to heal, to enrich, and to educate. What is the alternative? If we do not translate, then one of the most significant resources we have for conquering the isolation imposed by linguistic and cultural difference is squandered.

Translation is unnatural, but we do it because we must. Without translation the opportunity for information transfer is lost. The moral and aesthetic values of other cultures would be kept from us. The scientific discoveries and technical applications of other societies would be unknown. Of course, Venuti does not ask the translator to stop translating. He asks the translator to be aware of the potential for ethnocentric violence that translation carries. While translation's capacity for harm is undeniable, so is its ability to open the target culture to new ideas. Evolution and change in culture result from outside stimuli. The diffusion of innovation through texts is a constant pattern in culture. Translation has played a significant role in cultural change. It is true that translation can be used to suppress, but translation can also liberate. It can help to create new paradigms and new ways of living.

Translation has also enriched our languages. The lexical, syntactic, and stylistic inventories of languages have been as much enhanced by translation as they have been sullied by it. No modern language would be what it is today if not for translation. Think of the effect of the vast amount of translation from the classical languages into English. The repertoires, the structural distinctions, and the lexical systems of our modern languages have developed in significant reaction to linguistic contact through translation. Has this contact cheapened or trivialized the foreign *other*? Perhaps it has, but this is certainly not true in all cases. Cultural contact through translation has brought at least as many benefits as it has liabilities. This is yet another paradox of translation.

There are many texts which do not suffer appreciably in translation. Good examples are the pragmatic texts which constitute the bulk of the non-literary translator's work. What violence is done to the assembly manual for a child's bicycle when it is translated from Japanese into English? Should we ignore target-language textual expectations when we translate medical texts about the AIDS vaccine into other languages? Should a translator ignore the linguistic resources of the target language when he or she tries to make the text more fluent and accessible? Venuti indicts fluency in the target text because it lets the translation pass as an original text in the target language. He also indicts the use of translation resources, such as parallel texts, which make fluency possible. He assumes that linguistic and textual structure cannot be separated from the cultural values with which he is primarily concerned. Venuti sets his agenda when he states that the "point is rather to develop a theory and practice of translation that resists dominant target-language cultural values so as to signify the linguistic and cultural difference of the text" (Venuti 1991). In this statement he proposes a translation strategy opposed to fluency. The strategy uses non-fluent renderings of the target text to heighten the differences between source and target. Isn't this strategy based on the assumption that the target language is incapable of forms of expression which transfer and preserve the cultural values and unique ideas of the foreign culture? This bondage of language and cultural content denies the creative capacity of language. Resistive strategies try to preserve cultural difference. Isn't it possible for fluency and cultural difference to coexist? If translators understand cultural difference, why can't the resources of the target language be enlisted in its service? Maybe cultural values are lost because the translator does not understand them. Resistant translation is a denial of the power of language and the infinite novelty of expression that empowers every linguistic and textual system. Frankly, for most translators, this whole argument is a non-issue. Pragmatic texts make up the bulk of their work. Perhaps of greater concern for serious practitioners and eager users of translation is the great amount of translation which is neither destructive nor constructive, but simply awful.

Translation(s) and Text

We are aware that Venuti's call for resistive translation refers primarily to certain literary and cultural texts. We apologize for using his argument as a foil for our own. Venuti is correct in his analysis of the potential for harm in translation, and he focuses, as we do, on the effects of the translation process on textual form. Too many theorists focus on the translation process alone. They act as if process could be separated from text. The text is the central defining issue in translation. Texts and their situations define the translation process. We cannot generalize about translation without speaking of specific texts embedded in specific situations. There is no single translation process. There are many translation processes. Translation is an intersection of situation, translator competence, source text, and target text-to-be. There are translation situations where the destructive impact of translation on cultural values is not important. There are other situations where it may be the central issue. Some translation is critical and interpretive; it is not pragmatic. This kind of translation is driven by different motivating factors. The messages and forms of the texts are more closely connected. Other texts participate in practical communication. They exchange primarily value-free technical, scientific, and commercial information. The foreignness of the source text is not a benefit in these translations. Because most practical texts have a user orientation, the foreignness of the source text is an obstacle to overcome.

The translation situation always determines the set of translation strategies to be used. Translation appears to be a single process, but it actually refers to a set of situation-specific processes. Here we have another paradox of translation. Venuti makes the case himself when he says "as conceptual fields in which a translation is produced, fluency and resistancy ... are determined by the particular conjuncture where they are developed and used, and their ideological significance is not only defined in relation to that conjuncture, but influenced by the ideology of the source-language text that they process" (Venuti 1986, 191).

There are common features which all the possible translation processes share. There are also differences which distinguish them. Some differences are related to variations in the translation situation. Others are caused by the diverse information contents of source texts. Authors may have different intentions and readers can have different needs. There are always cultural differences in linguistic and conceptual systems. Finally, there are differences in what people expect translations to look like. One of the goals of translation studies should be to describe the varieties of translation that result from real combinations of these translation variables. Translation scholars need to look at real translation practice. Translation reality is rarely studied. Instead, we have studied armchair conceptualizations of translation. What translation scholars need to do, and have started to do over the past decade, is focus on the varieties of translation that actually exist. They need to look at what happens to source texts during translation and describe the influence of cultural, linguistic, and textual factors on the processes and results of translation.

Translation studies today is a cluster of overlapping perspectives. There is no unified way of approaching the study of translation. Practitioners and scholars stake out certain territories and construct their own isolated understandings of translation reality. Many of these perspectives are non-empirical. They are derived from disparate sources. Some come from models in other disciplines. Others come from metaphors and introspection. Each perspective emphasizes a different aspect of translation. Translation invites and recommends a variety of theoretical and methodological responses.

For instance, a scholar may focus on the source text in its sociocultural setting. This source-centered perspective will focus on the domestication of the source text by the target language. The translator plays the role of linguistic lion tamer. From this perspective, resistive translation makes sense. The utility of resistive translation dissipates when the perspective shifts. Resistant translation cannot be proposed as a universal strategy, but there are translation situations and translation needs which call for it. The utility of resistive translation rests primarily on text-ideological considerations, not pragmatic ones. The use of the technique is situation dependent. It requires a translation situation which places social concerns (gender, class, ethnicity) and awareness of the other (opacity of the text) above other concerns (readability, acceptability, informativity). A major problem with resistive translation is that by denying fluency and, by extension, the textuality of the target, the resistive translator runs the risk of producing non-texts which can seem very much like bad translations. How do we tell the difference? One possible answer is that resistive translation produces "something that cannot be confused with either the source-language text or a text written originally in the target language." The translation contains a "use of language that resists easy reading according to contemporary standards—that will make visible the intervention of the translator..."(Venuti 1986, 190). Venuti's idea of a discrete "use of language" implies that even resistive translation produces a systematic textual effect. It produces an "unnatural," but usable, text for a trained and attentive reader.

We must understand what a text is before we can think about translating one. The way we translate must proceed from a consideration of the source text and the translation situation. Because there are many texts and many potential reasons to translate them, there are many ways to translate. This volume is called *Translation as Text* because translation does not pre-exist. Translation is not brought to the text and then applied to it. It is a textual process that starts with the source text and is managed by the translator to produce a target text. The translator manages translation as a textual process meant to induce one text from another. In most cases of technical and commercial translation, the text that is induced should be a fluent text in a target language. In other cases, it may be an opaque resistive text, induced as a special response to a particular conjuncture of translation variables. Translation variables are primarily textual variables. The translator must learn to account for these variables in the process of translation. In the third chapter of this volume we turn to a detailed explanation of the textual variables that influence translation.

Thus, unnaturalness and necessity, loss and gain, destruction and harmony, integration and difference, are all properties of translation. They define its essential paradoxes. The study of translation should include an account of how these seemingly incompatible and divergent properties are mediated in the target text. Because translation is simultaneously a *process* and a *result*, there is a product whose success or failure can be evaluated. We can judge how the translator has responded to the demands of the translation situation. The translator always has choices to make. He or she has to cope with cultural difference and linguistic incompatibility. Translators have to master the difficulties of navigating messages to a foreign linguistic shore. The history of translation is full of examples of great triumph and shameful failure in this endeavor.

Unity and Difference in Translation Studies

Reflection on translation is almost as old as translation itself. The most articulate and thoughtful translators have considered the different ways to bridge the gulf between source and target text. They have reflected on the processes of translation. A translator usually begins the translation process by appraising the situation. Who wants the text? What do they need it for? Having appraised the situation, the translator may then apply certain operations to the text, thus initiating the actual work of translation. The process yields a translation result which is the target text. This triad of situation, process, and result is part of a specific kind of textual process. The translation process involves comprehending the source text and *retextualizing* it as a target text under specific conditions. Translation studies should be the rigorous observation and empirical description of how this retextualization is accomplished. It should include an account of the specific variables that influence the translation process. These variables might include, but are not limited to:

1. the systemics of the language pairs involved
2. the textual characteristics of the source and target texts
3. the situation, intentions, purposes, and needs of the target reader
4. differences in cultural, social, and communicative practices
5. cultural differences in knowledge organization
6. the extent and organization of shared knowledge
7. the textual expectations of the text reader
8. the information contents of the source text
9. the acceptability constraints on the target text

An ideal translation studies should investigate actual translation behavior. It should describe the ways that translators respond to variability in the translation situation. Finally, translation studies should explain actual translation products (target texts) as a function of the translation situation and translation behaviors performed in response to it.

Scholars have propagated endless lists of rules about how to translate. Many of these declarations are *prescriptive*, in that they claim to tell us how to translate. Translation studies in its empirical form is primarily *descriptive* and should be based on the observation of translation practice. As an empirical science, it has two objectives. It seeks to identify regularities in the way that translators respond to specific translation situations, and it seeks to identify regularities in the results of that response. A prescriptive translation didactics could emerge from this empirical approach but is not entailed by it. The ideal content for a translation didactics, however, would be a set of heuristics derived from an understanding of effective practice.

Because of the sheer volume of translation today, the amount of knowledge about the everyday practice of translation is impressive. It has become a veritable embarrassment of riches. On the basis of the burgeoning practice of translation, one would expect to develop a coherent, empirical body of opinion about translation. The empirical source material, what Toury has called the "observable facts" of translation, is available (Toury 1982). Yet, this body of agreed opinion on translation has not emerged. The sheer magnitude of the task of translation and the seemingly innumerable ways to approach it have resulted in the deplorable situation where "translators have freely contradicted one another about almost every aspect of their art" (Savory 1968, 9).

Some scholars have focused on the results of translation, others have focused on linguistic relationships, and still others have focused on what is lost from the source text. Over the past several years, there has been an attempt to consolidate all of the various approaches to translation into the field of *translation studies*. The discipline that is taking shape is an empirical discipline. The development of this new discipline is not unexpected. It is the result of an historical ferment in the discipline and is an attempt to bring unity out of disunity. The evolution of translation studies has been marked by several recognizable trends. This volume is not a history of translation studies, but two of these trends merit some discussion. One development is the shrinking role of linguistics as the intellectual basis for translation studies. The other trend is an increase in theoretical particularism. These two trends are primarily responsible for the current lack of consensus in translation studies.

Much early work in translation studies is rooted in the linguistic tradition. To linguistically oriented scholars, translators are simply a special class of speakers. Their competence is an analogue of the competence of the speakers of the source and target languages. Linguistic approaches, however they vary in detail, suffer from the delusion that translation can be assumed to be normal communication in two languages. Any practicing translator would tell us that the competence of a language mediator is quite different from the competence of a normal bilingual. Translation is not a mere cognitive bridge between two competences. Bilinguals, as a rule, make use of their linguistic competences only when appropriate communication situations arise. There is a linguistic division of labor. They may converse in one language at home and in the other language at school or work. They would normally never communicate the same content, or "say the same things" in both languages. Their command of two language systems has evolved as a functional phenomenon that will disintegrate as soon as communicative needs change and make the second linguistic competence superfluous.

Translation is a communicative activity that, while it may ideally presuppose the bilingual's double competence, calls for additional competences. The translator or interpreter must communicate a single textual content in a second text. Unlike the bilingual, the translator must "say the same thing" in both languages. Translation recasts the original message in a new linguistic form. The recasting is done for different people, after an unavoidable time lag, and at a different place. Translation is displaced and disjointed communication. In a way, the translator shares Hamlet's dilemma. But, luckily, it is not the world, but only its mirror, language, that the translator has to put right for his or her audience: *Language is out of joint; O cursed spite that ever I was born to set it right.*

Being able to "set things right" involves more than just linguistics. We cannot make the simple assumption that translation is a linguistic process. This will not lead to a better understanding of how effective translations work. A better understanding of translation cannot come from any approach that focuses on a single aspect, such as linguistic form, of a more complex phenomenon. Translation is bound to the communicative roles that translations and their source language progenitors play in social life. Translations are texts, and translation is a textual process in which linguistic form and process are incorporated. Texts are the building blocks of communication in general, and of translation in particular. The text has to be considered the primary object of translation study.

The historical debate over the role of linguistics has had both positive and negative effects. Our embrace of linguistics was not just a result of the linguistic parentage of our discipline; it was also motivated by the need for a systematic approach. Just because linguistics was not the systematic model we needed is no reason to reject a broader and more comprehensive approach to translation. The current interest that translation studies has in a systematic approach is a legacy of its linguistic heritage. This need for a systematics can be met by an empirical translation science. More damaging to the development of modern translation studies is the non-empirical tradition which developed when formal linguistics and descriptive linguistics parted company. Translation studies should be based on the observation of practice. Like the early ethnolinguists, such as Franz Boas, who observed language in use, translation scholars should observe the indigenous performance and natural uses of translation. Unlike speech, translation is not a natural competence. It is a result of experience, training, and the feedback effects of client-translator or translator-reader interaction.[4] The hypotheses, models, and theories developed in translation studies should be based on data collected from the body of translation practice. As such, data collection in translation studies should be at least partly ethnographic. By detaching reflection on translation from the observation of practice, the linguists of translation created the basis for division in the discipline.

We have said that a second source of the lack of consensus in translation studies is theoretical particularism. Particularism can be defined as the creation of multiple "global" theoretical constructs based on purely "local" understandings of a phenomenon. When this happens in a discipline, as for instance when theory is divorced from the observation of reality, then confusion and ambiguity arise. When translation scholars write about translation there is no guarantee that they share the same underlying concepts and assumptions. At translation conferences and in the literature, there is an enormous amount of frustrating miscommunication. More scholars than ever are dealing seriously with the subject of translation. While there are growing areas of agreement, the state of translation studies is far from satisfactory. What authors are writing, and translation teachers are teaching, is often contradictory. The concept of translation is as ambiguous as it is paradoxical. The ambiguity behind our miscommunication comes from several sources. A first source is the process-result question. When we discuss translation, are we viewing it primarily as a process? Or are we viewing it as a result? Another source of ambiguity is the fact we are a young discipline. Young disciplines have competing paradigms with imprecise, dynamic, and overlapping terminologies and concept systems. The last source of ambiguity is the text-bound nature of translation. Every translation (product) is the result of a process (translation) which begins with a dynamic configuration of source text, translation situation, and translator competence. All of the translation variables we listed before are active. Every translation, in its broad outlines, is like all other translations. But, in its particulars, each translation is always different. The translator makes strategic choices and realizes from a range of textual possibilities a single target text. This inherent dynamism always presents a different face of translation to the translator or scholar. There is disarray in the discipline because translators fail to define the differences in the translations (processes and results) that they study. Students of translation, describing only one part or kind of translation, are like the blind men and the elephant. They think they are describing the whole elephant when they are only touching its ear or tail. Then they proceed to propose their perfectly legitimate, but particular, statements as global ones.

Is there a way to improve this state of affairs? The first thing we must do is re-attach theory and practice by basing empirical theory on the direct observation of practice; then we must proceed to remove the ambiguities that come from theoretical particularism. It might be possible to remove some of the ambiguities by specifying the particular context of every discussion. Here we are reminded of Venuti's call for translators to describe their understandings and strategies in translators' prefaces. This approach would perhaps be a practical solution in many individual situations and would clarify the issues for the readers of a particular book or paper. On closer examination, such a particularistic approach would not be very constructive for translation studies and would lead to a proliferation of idiosyncratic views of translation. There needs to be a set of common methods which can be applied to all of the different perspectives. If the goal of translation scholarship is the development of a systematic empirical discipline, then every scholar who contributes ideas should clearly define the approach and perspective being taken. It is important to move away from impressionistic ideas about an already vague subject. Translation scholars must be explicit about their perspectives. Are they commenting on translation behavior, translation result, or on the translation situation? Scholars should be explicit about the observations and data which they use to support their claims. Our call for explicitness includes revealing the methods that were used in gathering data and generating hypotheses. It calls for announcing the motivations for the research being conducted. When we all start speaking the same language to one another, it may be that what appears to be an infinite number of approaches to translation is actually a finite set of variations on a few distinct themes.

Models of Translation

Analysis in any discipline involves decomposing the object of study. Some features are selected for study and are brought to the foreground. Others, equally important, are relegated to the background. Hjelmslev has discussed this selection process and related it to the semiotic concept of pertinence (Greimas and Courtes 1982, 31). The selection of those aspects of a phenomenon that one will study is made on the basis of a set of research parameters. The research parameters reflect the pertinence of the phenomenon to the scholar. Research parameters in translation studies might include the following:

1. the application domain (practice, pedagogy, criticism, automation)
2. the point of textual reference (source-centered, translation-centered, target-centered)

3. the systemic focus (linguistic system, value system, knowledge system, text system, cognitive system, political system)
4. the object focus (source text, translation, parallel text)
5. the activity focus (text comprehension, text production, translation strategy, cognition)
6. the research method (case study, experiment, textual analysis, participant observation)

In translation studies the potential for misunderstanding is not just the result of a divergence of research interest. Such divergence is characteristic of research. It is also the result of a failure to clarify the *research parameters* active when a complex object of study is partitioned for research purposes.

Translation studies today is characterized by alternative perspectives on translation. They have their origins in different research aims and interests. Different motivations for research and the varied prospects for utilizing its results produce a natural partitioning of translation studies. These different partitions can be referred to as *models of translation*. A model is a conceptual construct. It is a logically connected set of conceptualizations of an object of study. It may also be a hypothetical construct. This means that the model asserts something about empirical (translational) reality which the researcher intends to prove. As a hypothetical conceptual construct, the model claims to have descriptive and explanatory power. It is important to note that models are not theories. Models are like hypotheses. They only claim to explain and describe reality. A model cannot become a theory without providing evidence which supports its claim to explanatory power. Such evidence is often lacking in translation studies. In the place of empirical verification, many of these models depend on weaker forms of authority: the sophistication of the argument, the status of the model's author, or the coherence of formal systems. More condemning, the relationship between translation theory and translation practice is weak, as evidenced by the small number of empirical investigations reported in the literature.

Identifying the research parameters which motivate the different models of translation is a first step toward clarification. Two divergent views of translation may not really be in opposition. They may simply focus on different aspects of a larger phenomenon. Still, the broader discipline of translation studies needs a conceptual baseline. We argue that the textual approach to translation can serve as that baseline. Without an integrating concept we run the risk that translation will be understood only in parts, and never as a whole. If there are no integrating concepts, there can be no hope of an integrated or unified theory of translation. An integrated theory would bring the various models of translation and the various kinds of translation together in a more encompassing theoretical structure.

Building models without a common set of concepts has led to the fracturing of translation studies noted recently by Newmark and earlier by Savory. In a recent paper, Newmark has maintained that "an integrated theory of translation is not feasible" (Newmark 1990, 711). Newmark continues to say that "all theories have their uses; when they are claimed to be exclusive or monopolistic, they become pernicious dogma." Newmark is right about dogma. It has no place in translation studies and cannot exist in any empirically based discipline. He goes too far when he claims that an integrated theory of translation is not possible.[5] Each approach to translation can validate itself. It can achieve validity by carefully selecting its research aims and using a rigorous methodo-critical system in the description of the phenomenon within that selection. The scope, and therefore the explanatory power, of the model of translation is restricted to the elements subjected to analysis. It is not necessarily the case that an integrated theory is impossible. Simply because some approaches to translation have decided to focus on a restricted set of elements does not mean that a more comprehensive and meaningful set of features cannot be constructed. This could be done by merging the common conceptual elements of the various models and accounting for the areas of difference.

An integrated approach requires an integrating concept. We have proposed the text as an integrating concept. In translation we are concerned with three incarnations of the text. There is the source text and there is the target text. The third text is what we call the *virtual translation*. The virtual translation is a composite of the possible relations between a source text and a range of potential target texts. It is a mental model of the elements and relations which exist in the mental space between real source and not-yet-realized target. The translator factors the conditions of the translation situation into her understanding of the source text to create this mental model. He or she negotiates a target text from the mental model using the procedures available in her translator's competence. What the layman calls "the translation" is the target text, the linguistic incarnation of a virtual translation that was a work-in-progress until it was delivered to its reader. We call this cognitive structure a virtual translation because we want to emphasize its mental nature. It is a mental construct only progressively committed to paper. The virtual translation is always constrained by the source text and by the textual expectations of the reader. Even though it is a mental construct, it is text-like. The concept of virtual translation is one that emphasizes the fact that the translator works with a mental representation. The representation is anchored by a source text and oriented in its progressive elaboration by the determinants of the translation situation. As it emerges into linguistic reality in the target culture, it is increasingly controlled by the target culture's linguistic and textual systems. The virtual translation includes a number of interdependent constituents and relations. Relations in the virtual translation are between the elements of the two linguistic systems and between elements of the source text and the target text *in potentio*. The mental representation includes the propositional content and the illocutionary force of the messages underlying the source text. It includes the pragmatic conditions surrounding the text in the source and target communities.

In the remainder of this volume we shall examine the significant relations that affect the virtual translation in its journey to target text. Specifically, we shall address seven parameters that determine the textual character of the virtual translation as it evolves in translation practice: intentionality, acceptability, situationality, informativity, coherence, cohesion, and intertextuality. These textual characteristics may be manipulated in favor of the target culture or in resistance to it. They are the determining features of textuality, and therefore, of translation. Because the virtual translation is influenced by many communicative and functional elements, this object of translation studies truly reaches into the semiotic domains of semantics and pragmatics. It accounts for the authors and readers of translations. It accounts for their knowledge, thoughts, and feelings; it includes their aims, intentions, needs and expectations.[6]

The process of translation is a process of decision-making. It is a set of procedures and strategies for making judgments when selecting the optimal choice from a range of potential equivalents. A theory of translation should attempt to understand how that decision-making is accomplished. How is the mental representation of the virtual translation constructed and how does it emerge as a target language text? A theory of translation should explicate how the professional translator moves from the concrete source text, to the construction of the virtual translation, to producing the most appropriate target text. It should explicate the factors that play into the decision-making, including communicative function, target language textual style, potential audience, and the requirements of the host culture and linguistic system.

No integrated theory of translation should concentrate on just one of these issues. It is legitimate, however, for partial theories of translation to circumscribe their areas of interest. In the following chapters, we will expand on the notion of translation as text by showing how the text as (virtual) translation, and the related concepts of textual meaning and communicative value, can function as integrating conceptual structures in translation studies. Although we argue that an integrated theory of translation is possible, we recognize that before we can proceed with our argument, we should describe some of the partial theories that have preoccupied translation studies to date: the critical, practical, linguistic, text-linguistic, sociocultural, computational, and psycholinguistic models. This inventory of research perspectives is not just an authorial strategy. It is a necessary preparation for any serious discussion at this stage in the development of our common discipline. The order in which we review the models does not indicate any order of priority.[7]

The Critical Model

The critical model normally presupposes a finished translation. The translation exists in time and space. The critic's objective is evaluative commentary. This perspective on translation is result-oriented and static. There is no inherent interest in understanding how the translation was accomplished or in understanding how the translator used particular translation procedures. The critic orients himself to the results of translation, not its processes. More sophisticated critical models may assess the degree of equivalence between a translation and the original text. What often occurs, however, is that a critic loses sight of the source text as a concrete linguistic entity. The primary object is the target text. If the source text is available (and comprehensible) to the critic, he may use it in analysis. But there is no doubt that the major factor determining a critic's acceptance of a translation is the translation product viewed as a text in its own right.

There are many variations of the critical model of translation. These models develop and change over time. They are conditioned by distinct historical, social, and individual factors. Two features of the critical model, the degree of subjectivity, and the dominance of the target language, are directly related to the critic's ability to access the source text and make genuine comparisons. The two skills, however, that would enhance the reliability of the critical model are least developed by some practitioners of the approach. These critics, primarily publishers' readers and book reviewers, concentrate largely on the acceptability of the text in the target language. There is a difference between this literary criticism of translations and *translation criticism*. The first focuses on the literary or textual qualities of the work as it exists in translation. The translation is judged on its own merits as a target language text. Translation criticism, on the other hand, appraises the text *as a translation*.

There are various realizations of the critical model that merge into the other models of translation. For instance, criticism, or rather correction, is an integral part of translation teaching (the practical model). It is used in translation classes with translation students. More often than not, it is applied to parts of translated texts. This approach deals with effects emanating from the target text. These effects may be subjective ("it sounds wrong") or the result of the violation of more conventional linguistic and textual norms. Another important variety of the critical model is translation revision performed as quality control. In this case it is carried out by a better or more qualified second translator who invests her greater experience and her broader knowledge of the target audience in this demanding task.

Translation criticism should always be comparative, maintaining the source and target texts as a pair. A full development of the critical model would have to develop a research methodology which is essentially contrastive. It would have to merge translation values, translation results, and source and target language values.

There is a unique kind of critical translation analysis which is not comparative. It focuses on the source text to be translated and deals primarily with defective texts. It does not regard the original as inviolable; it urges the translator to look for defects. Translators in industry constantly complain that "the one big problem has to do with the quality of the source texts—source texts that are simply not satisfactory as departure points for the purposes to be served by the corresponding target texts" (Berglund 1990, 146). The most common flaws, which often go undetected if the conscientious translator does not interfere, are obscurity, inconsistency, and interference.[8]

The critical model, with its retrospective thrust, starts out from the product. It concentrates on translation as result, not as process. The proponents of this model still have to take into account the kind of translation that was done. Different types of texts presuppose different translation techniques and different criteria for revision or criticism. Hence, the critical model of translation studies presupposes a variety of critical methods based on the types of text involved. The criteria established for assessing industrial translations are bound to be different from the criteria used by a critic of literary translations. The critical model is an indispensable part of a global view of translation. The critical model focuses on textual acceptability. Acceptability is a defining characteristic of textuality. Because of this intrinsic link to textuality the critical model can participate fruitfully in the more global text-based conception of translation that we propose.

The Practical Model

The practical model of translation takes the source text as a point of departure. The goal is an understanding of the target text through a study of the processes of translation (translation behaviors, translation strategies) that lead to an acceptable translation. Where the critical model was retrospective the practical model is prospective. The objects of study are the declarative knowledge and procedural knowledge necessary for the translator to do his or her work. The practical model involves a thorough analysis of the source text and its context. The major practical objective is determining how to transfer the contents of the source into the target. The practical model assesses latent translations in the source text and studies the transfer mechanisms used to bring one of these into target text reality. The practical model emphasizes the construction of the virtual translation and the realization of a target text from it. The critical model, on the other hand, focuses on target text realities and only presupposes a potential source. Thus, the practical model is also based on the integrating concept of the text.

The practical model is not static, but dynamic. It is not easy to characterize this model of translation with a single term. It is embraced by practitioners, researchers, teachers, and students of translation. Because of these different users, it is possible to identify several different sub-models, including the practical, the teaching, and the learning approaches. As a result, the model exists in various degrees of sophistication. The designation *practical* emphasizes the fact that this approach to translation studies focuses on the processes of human translation practice. It is a way of looking at translation if you actually have to do it. Another appropriate designation might be *performative model*. All of the sub-models share the prospective interest, but they play different performative roles. These different roles result in the use of different sets of declarative and procedural resources to get practical results.

Our differentiation of the sub-models raises an interesting point. It shows that *models* are not entirely the property of the researcher. The real conceptualizations that practitioners have of the translation process are also models. What is often overlooked by the translation scholar is that *practitioners* also have a conception of the translation process that guides them. This informal translation model is a first-order model of translation. It is not completely conscious. Often it is latent, but detectable and quite consistent. Of course, this everyday knowledge tends to be less explicitly formulated. Mostly, it is not put into words at all. The experienced translator, the successful teacher, and the gifted student realize practical models of translation in strategies and tactics of translation that defy a clear-cut order. Nevertheless, they appear as regular patterns under empirical observation. Evidence of good translations over the centuries proves that there have always been practical models.

As practical models are formalized by rigorous processes of observation, comparison, and empirical study, patterns will emerge. First-order practical models will yield second-order practical models for teaching translation and for improving practice. The relationship between first-order and second-order understandings of translation is a significant issue that we will take up again in our discussion of translation theory.

The Linguistic Model

The linguistic model of translation makes statements about the linguistic mechanisms involved in the transfer or replacement of source language signs by target language signs. This approach treats translation as a specific, perhaps unique, type of language use. It does not consider external or *extralinguistic* factors such as critical norms or the constraints of practice. It concentrates, instead, on systemic relationships between the source and target languages. The model studies the linguistic resources of the source and target languages and the mechanisms available in the target language for overcoming the structural differences between source and target that appear in translation. The linguistic model investigates the transfer potentials of words and constructions and tries to establish correspondence rules between languages. Correspondence rules may obtain at various linguistic levels.

They may obtain between source and target language words and between source and target language grammatical structures. They may also refer to larger structures. Most correspondence rules are of a complex grammatico-lexical type. The corpus of knowledge about the rule-governed linguistic behavior of the translation pair is the basis of the contrastive linguistics of translation.[9]

There is also a more general linguistic model that is often taken to represent the linguistic model proper. Sometimes called "translation linguistics" (Jäger 1975) or "linguistic theory of translation" (Catford 1965), this abstract branch of translation studies is even thought to be the same thing as translation theory. In our opinion, equating any form of the linguistic model with a full translation theory is not justified. There is more than just linguistics involved in translation. Further, this identification wrongly suggests that linguistic theory-making is the main part of translation studies. It treats the linguistic model as the chief pretender to the throne of translation theory, when it is just one important model among many.

Some scholars have claimed that the linguistic model differs from the other models of translation because it is not an *applied model*. Because the model deals with the systemic relations between languages, it is highly abstract. The abstract nature and formality of the model is thought to set it apart from the applied models, to make it more theoretical. In the context of translation studies, the binary distinction between the term *applied* and its presumed opposite, *theoretical*, is an artifice. It equates theory with abstractness and application with concreteness. In other words, the more we deal with language as system (and the less we deal with concrete translation behaviors), the more theoretical our model. This distinction obscures the relationship between theory and practice. The practical model, which certainly deals with applied problems of language in use, is just as theoretical as the linguistic model. Theory-building is a process of observation, concept formation, hypothesis construction, and verification which may be applied in any discipline. Theory-building proceeds from the observation of the concrete and is a process of making and verifying generalizable statements. These statements may refer to the structural features of language or to translation practice.

Further, the linguistic model of translation is precisely about understanding how language can be applied by translators. The contrastive linguistics of translation is an applied linguistics, in that it studies the linguistic correspondences that actually occur or can occur in translation practice. Any model of translation that claims to deal with translation is dealing with *language in use*. Translation practice is the application of a translator's knowledge to problems of intercultural communication. This includes the translator's knowledge of the paired linguistic systems. Translation practice results in texts. The application of translational competence to text production is a form of work in all but the most scholarly of situations, and is a legitimate object of translation theory. Thus, all models of translation are "applied," to the extent they study a unique form of applied communicative problem-solving. If they state the results of their studies in the form of descriptive and explanatory constructs, then they are also theoretical.

The linguistic model's abstract and formal nature is partly traceable to its concern with linguistic meaning. The linguists of translation investigate how meanings are carried over from one language to another. The reconstruction of meaning is understood as a form of language recoding. From this perspective, translation is primarily a research and rewriting activity. Source linguistic units are rewritten as their target language equivalents. Their respective meanings are held relatively constant. Meaning invariance between source and target language signs and sign constellations is a first principle in this model. Meaning invariance allows greater possibilities of formal description.

Of course, scholars who embrace the linguistic approach to translation bring with them their views on meaning. As a consequence, they interpret equivalence in a variety of ways. Their understanding of equivalence depends on how far they presuppose a repertoire of semantic universals rich enough and distinguished enough to match the meaning gradients between the simple and complex signs of the two languages.[10]

What current linguistic models describe is not just the matching of discrete linguistic elements below the sentence boundary. It is the genuine reconstruction of utterance meanings. In this respect, the linguistic model goes beyond contrastive grammar and lexicology. The study of the variable mechanisms for reconstructing meaning during translation involves the *semantic quanta* carried over during restructurings and relexicalizations. There is no doubt that any attempt to measure linguistic meaning transfer of this kind presupposes some form of universal semantics.

The linguistic model is an extension of linguistics applied to bilingually mediated communication. It is a comparative and descriptive model which comes in a variety of forms. All of these forms share a common feature: they focus on the formulation of objective statements about the systematic correlation of patterns of source and target language sign sequences. All source-target differences that occur in translation are traceable to differences in the two language systems. From this point of view, translation studies is nothing but an extension of systemic linguistics. Interlinguistic relationships are a justified concern of professional linguists, and in this respect, they represent basic research. They contribute to our theoretical understanding of the way languages work. It is unclear whether the linguistic model is of use for practicing translators. The linguistic model of translation has been rejected by some practicing translators and by proponents of other models of translation. The model has been characterized as being too abstract and removed from practical application. It is only in this sense, the sense of practical utility, that the linguistic model is not an applied model. The linguistic approach has even been attacked as counterproductive (Berglund 1990; Newmark 1991).

There are two senses of the word *applied* which can be used with the linguistic model. The first is "having practical utility in the teaching or improvement of translation practice." The second is "examining, describing, and making objective statements about the interaction of linguistics systems as they occur in the applied activity of translation." The linguistic model is applied in the second sense, but not in the first. The generalizations of the linguistic theorists of translation may or may not be helpful for adherents of the critical or practical models. They may be impartial with respect to any potential application. This impartiality is reflected in the way linguistic statements on translation are formulated. The model of translation propounded by linguists cannot possibly stand in any direct relationship to the other models. Scholars using the other models must account for the linguistic aspects of translation within their own research agendas and borrow what they need from the contrastive linguistics of translation. The linguistic model is a legitimate way of looking at translation for its own, linguistic, sake. It tells us something about linguistic reality but not necessarily something about translation reality. At the very least, it is an important part of the knowledge background of someone who wants to take on translation as a profession, as the knowledge of certain sciences is essential for the aspiring physician.

The Text-linguistic Model

The text-linguistic model of translation maintains that an original text and a translation are different not only because their sentences are different (having been determined by the linguistic rules of two different language systems), but also because there are constraints operating at a level beyond the sentence. A traditional contrastive linguistic approach cannot explain these suprasentential *textual* factors.

Another motivation for the development of the text-linguistic model of translation comes from the practical experience of doing translations and teaching translation students. If we look at good translations and compare them with dreary dictionary-bound, grammar book-inspired, linguistically correct translations, the limitations of the linguistic approach will be apparent. The lexical items, syntactic structures, and textual properties that make a successful translation are not necessarily those a contrastive linguistic model might have predicted. The linguistic systems of the source and target cannot account for the pragmatically-motivated transformations and modifications made to a linguistically adequate target text. By *pragmatics* we refer to the various uses of language by speakers and writers in particular communicative situations (Neubert 1968b, 1973a). The translator must usually modify the source text using a variety of methods, including explicitation, deletion, and modulation in order to produce a more satisfactory and pragmatically adequate translation. This textually adequate translation is better than anything that could be produced using only the more evident equivalents suggested by a language-systemic model. Translations are more than duplications or restructurings of source language sequences. They represent configurations of *text sentences*. The sentence-by-sentence progression of a translation is determined by top-down processes driven by the conventions that obtain for a particular textual category in the target culture (Neubert 1988). The linguistic model presumes a bottom-up process which begins with words and their discrete meanings. Bottom-up translation can never yield acceptable target language texts.

In the text-linguistic model meaning is not sentence-bound. The model locates and distributes meaning equivalence throughout the text. Instead of being isolated in words and sentences, meaning is also carried globally in the text. What is actually carried over into the target text during translation is the composite semantic value and pragmatic function of the source text. With the global meaning of the original as the determining factor, the translation is reconstructed as a new semantic and pragmatic totality in the target language community. The surface structure of the reconstruction is not a sentence by sentence rendering of the original. It is a top-down recreation of the text through the purposeful selection of target language resources. The selection of linguistic resources is guided by the virtual translation (mental model) in the translator's mind. The linguistic resources of the target clothe the virtual translation and create the translation as physical text.

The model is called "text-linguistic" because it is a further development of the linguistic model. It reflects the expansion of translation studies into discourse analysis and pragmatics. The text-linguistic model differs from the linguistic model in its broader, text-based conception of meaning and its more realistic formulation of the notion of translation equivalence. It locates equivalence at a textual and communicative level, not at the sentential and lexical level. The text-linguistic approach provides more powerful analytic tools for the study of translation than sentential linguistics has provided. This analytic power has its price. Because of the systemic relationships between source and target languages, semantic correspondences between individual sentences in source and target texts are quite predictable in a linguistic model. The similarities and differences between the textual worlds of the source and target cultures are less defined and less predictable. This is, of course, part of the nature of texts. They are not entirely the product of linguistic rules. Most translations have to simulate the typical textual profiles of the target culture. The rules that will show a translator how to produce the right textual profile every time have not been written yet. The temptation is to envy the predictability that the sentence-bound linguistic model can provide. There are, however, limits to this predictability; as one moves beyond the sentence boundary, the linguistic model cannot predict what actual, high-quality professional translations will look like (Neubert 1987; Neubert 1989, 63).

The linguistic and text-linguistic models treat meaning differently. In the text-linguistic model, translation does not involve the transfer of meanings. It is, rather, the *communicative values* of the source text that are transferred. The term refers to the communicative contextualization of words and meanings in discourse. Communicative values are meaning composites seen entirely at a textual level and in communicative context. One might argue, as is fashionable in some linguistics circles, that we should expand the boundaries of linguistics to include all of the variables associated with human communication. One might then dispense with a separate text-linguistic model, and include it as a special form of the linguistic model. As it stands, it is better to consider the text-linguistic model of translation as a distinct approach. Its frame of reference is not the linguistic system but the textual systems of two communicating communities. Textual systems are complex sets of expectations text users have about what texts should be like. With an understanding of these expectations in mind, the translator engages in a textual process of transfer and text production. In the translator's eyes, the target text is a text induced as a response to another text. The translator facilitates the textuality of the target text by mediating the two textual systems. Translations according to this model are *text-induced text productions.*

The Sociocultural Model

There is another model of translation that de-emphasizes the linguistic system. The model does recognize the verbal substratum of translation, but defines translation primarily as an attempt at cross-cultural communication. In this model, texts are seen as unique products of the history and social structure of a particular culture. Because their contexts are unique, texts are not repeatable. An extreme version of this model leads to translation nihilism. Translation would be impossible. Less radical views would propose specific strategies to prevent sociocultural loss during translation. In the sociocultural model target texts are either not translatable or are corruptions of the original sources. Some proponents of the sociocultural model will admit translatability. They simply think that translation's ability to overcome historical and sociocultural barriers is limited. These translation skeptics will sometimes refer to "untranslatable" texts. Most of their examples are texts for which the target culture has no need. The texts have no counterparts in the other culture. In these cases, the textual situations are incompatible.

The socioculturalists particularly oppose the idea of translation equivalence; they see it as an illusion. They perceive translations as glimpses into alternate realities where perceptions are different. If this otherness is translated away, they argue, then genuine translation is betrayed. Given this position, it follows that translations should always be recognized as surrogates. What the readers of the surrogate texts retrieve from them is never the "real thing." This contradicts the text-linguistic model where the motivation is communion with the textual conventions of the target community. The sociocultural approach maintains that translations should always read like translations. The target text must be an oblique rendering of the source. Points of sociocultural and linguistic difference are maintained as markers of its sojourn into alien territory. Nevertheless, the rules of the target linguistic system still apply because the result must be minimally accessible to the target audience. Sociocultural translation creates surface understanding on the basis of linguistic sequences that are formally correct, but leave the reader unsettled. The model produces target texts that are an unnatural hybrid of target language and source text. Many proponents of this school believe this is as it should be.

The sociocultural target text is composed of familiar words and phrases, interspersed with untranslatable borrowings from the original. A translation's effect on the target culture is always hard to predict. The basic tenet of the sociocultural model is that this effect must be different from the effect of the original on its native audience. Translations and their readers have to live with this state of affairs. By compensating for the unavoidable divergence of source and target culture, and by meddling with their linguistic consequences in the target text, sociocultural theorists argue that translators prevent readers from appreciating the source culture. In their view, mediated translations do away with the original author and place too much responsibility for the target text in the hands of the translator. A variation of this approach (Venuti's resistive translation) calls, ironically, for more translator influence. Venuti urges translators to discard their "invisibility" (Venuti 1986). These arguments are a clear break from the more pragmatic line of the textually oriented translation scholar. Clearly, one's model of translation shapes one's ideas of what a translation should be and what must be done to produce one.

A choice of the sociocultural model over the text-linguistic model is not a choice between two global models. The sociocultural approach is clearly only applicable to certain kinds of texts. It is useful in situations where the violation of textual conventions in the target language is warranted by an overriding concern with the value of source language linguistic form as a carrier of cultural value. The text created in the target language is, however, still a text. It is an artificial ideotext or "opaque" text created by the translator as a specific vehicle for cultural values. Such texts would rarely be used for more mundane and practical kinds of translations. These opaque texts, unless they are completely idiosyncratic, display their own textual profile. This profile might be a hybrid of the conjoined textual systems of the two cultures. It could be an adaptation of the source language textual system to the target culture. The text is still the central issue in this model, just as it is in the critical, practical, and text-linguistic models.

THE COMPUTATIONAL MODEL

The five models discussed so far presume that translation is a completely human process. Since the earliest days of the digital computer, however, attempts have been made to translate by or with the assistance of computing machines. There are really two computational models of translation, machine translation and computer-assisted translation. Machine translation requires very little, if any, human assistance during the actual translation phase. Computer-assisted translation leaves the translation process in the hands of the human translator but provides intelligent support for his or her activities.

Machine translation reduces the processes and procedures of translation to formal representations. The representations are not based on human translation behavior. It is quite possible to get reasonable results without using human-derived algorithms. Texts are translated by substitution and transposition; the process is controlled by rules that act directly on the character strings in the source text. A human-programmed expression of a linguistic model underlies the translation software, but the actual transfer does not involve human participation. Machine translation is based upon formal representation; translation equivalence is reduced to formal equivalence. This equivalence-based recoding of linguistic form is rarely adequate. Pre-editors and post-editors have to edit the machine product for the human reader. Strangely enough, human post-editing can improve machine translation; in complex systems with knowledge acquisition capabilities it may be possible to analyze the revisions that are made by pre- and post-editors. The analysis of revisions can provide new rules to be added to the translation rule-base. By investing their expertise, translators can improve the set of transfer rules. An evolving cycle of feedback and revision, with increasingly successful translation runs, could produce more sophisticated machine translation systems. The machine translation model parallels the linguistic model. The formal equivalences on which the machine relies are equivalences between the source and target languages. They are programmed as sets of rewrite rules triggered when the program encounters words and constructions and recognizes them as tokens of stored dictionary entries and programmed syntactic templates.

There are several approaches to machine translation. What they have in common is a reliance on formal transfer mechanisms. Some approaches use direct transfers between source and target language; others utilize an interlanguage. An interlanguage is a set of metalinguistic expressions which are used to mediate the different sign systems. As machine translation becomes more sophisticated, this interlanguage will include even greater amounts of semantic and pragmatic information. Machine translation could be enhanced by incorporating text-linguistic information. One could, for instance, qualify equivalence rules with text-type specific operators. The software would then automatically select those renderings typical of particular text types. The amount of editing would be greatly reduced. This refinement would be possible only in certain domains and with text types whose textual conventions are expressible as procedural or declarative knowledge. Corporate translation users will have to assume the development costs for such systems. Applications will only be feasible if there are large numbers of texts to be translated. Machine translation is clearly linked with high-volume specialized commercial and technical translation.

The machine translation model may be quite effective in these restricted applications. It can be effective even if it is not *psychologically valid*. It is enough that it be *structurally valid*. Structural validity means that the translation result is acceptable, but the process used to achieve it is not psychologically real. The machine translation model is not a model of translation activity, what a translator does. It is a formal model developed to achieve results. While it might be possible to design computer software that translates like human beings do, we might find that such formal representations are not as efficient as purely structural representations (Shreve 1990).

In the other computational model, computer-assisted translation, the computer is a tool for the human translator. The translator stays in control of the translation. The translator works within a software environment tailored to his or her work-style. The environment acts as an amplifier or prosthesis for the translator (Shreve 1991). The effective software design of computer-assisted translation environments requires empirical studies of translation behavior. Based on preliminary empirical work, the well-designed computer environment should support those areas of consultation and research which consume most of the translator's time. Computer assistance (excluding normal word-processing functions) involves five primary areas of reference support (Shreve 1990; Scherf 1990; Gommlich and Förster 1991):

1. terminological/lexical assistance
2. encyclopedic and knowledge-organizational assistance
3. text-typological and parallel text assistance
4. translation-strategic assistance
5. document management assistance

The translation-strategic component is a mechanism for recording and retrieving successful translation strategies. A properly designed system could capture effective solutions to typical translation problems and store them. Computer-assisted translation would include *translation expert systems* capable of providing intelligent decision support (Neubert 1986).

Both sub-models of computer translation require linguistic and translation expertise. Even though the machine translation model does not mimic the actual processes of human translation, the results of the translation are judged against human translations. The algorithms driving the machine translation may then be altered to provide more acceptable results. Both machine translation and computer-assisted translation involve decision-making. In the case of machine translation the computer makes decisions based on formal representations created to achieve end results. In computer-assisted translation decisions are made by human beings, using a knowledge support system designed to enhance the quality of the translations.

To a certain extent, translations produced by machine translation are accepted as unfinished products. They are a kind of raw material which a human translator or post-editor has to finish. Our ability to proceed beyond this raw material stage in machine translation is limited by our ability to understand and represent the translation process as a textual and not just a linguistic process. The limits are not technical limits. The knowledge needed to improve machine translation has not been captured in a formalism appropriate for automation.

The computational model contributes to a better understanding of the other models. The attempt to produce good translations by machine (or with machine support) presumes an appreciation for the important issues in translation. Both models are ultimately concerned with producing usable texts. Like the practical model, the computational model is pragmatic. The quest for better translations will push the computational models to find ways of dealing with textuality and the text production process. These models will also focus on the text and its textuality.

THE PSYCHOLINGUISTIC MODEL

No single model can deal with all aspects of translation. The six models discussed so far have not dealt specifically with the mental operations involved in the translation process. Translation in relation to other kinds of verbal processes is "a task that makes certain demands on the cognitive system" of its practitioners (Neubert 1991b). The psycholinguistic model is concerned with describing the cognitive aspects of the translation process. Translation teachers began this line of inquiry when they started to search for ways to adapt their teaching to reflect the cognitive demands translation made on their students. The psycholinguistic approach has outgrown this initial pedagogical perspective. It now deals with the general cognitive structure of translation, including the specific cognitive processes that are involved. The model attempts to isolate the cognitive factors and language processing strategies which characterize translation.[11] The primary research question in this model is: *What goes on in the mind of the translator?* (Krings 1986a).

The psycholinguistic perspective views translation as a "black box" in which cognitive processes occur. Toury (1982, 25) comments on the empirical implications of the psycholinguistic model:

> Translated texts and their constitutive elements are observational facts ... translation processes, those series of operations whereby actual translations are derived from actual source texts, though no doubt also empirical facts, and as such part of the object-level of translation studies, are nevertheless only indirectly available for study as a kind of 'black box'.

To uncover the cognitive processes hidden inside the black box, students of translation must use empirical methods, including experiments. This model, of the ones so far described, is the most overtly empirical. It has modeled its research agenda on psycholinguistics and the cognitive sciences.

One method for unveiling the contents of the black box is the think-aloud-protocol (TAP). These protocols capture the translator's reactions and commentaries as he or she reflects on the task at hand. They track the development of the text from its initial to its final version using the translator's verbalized self-commentary. A solely verbal protocol, however complex it may be, does not always pinpoint those concrete textual problems in the original or in the nascent target text that have prompted a particular reaction or comment. Some researchers have resolved this problem by using more sophisticated research methods. Video-cameras, for instance, have been used to record the rapid eye movements that accompany translation; they are used to index the respective portions of the protocol to specific segments of the source and target texts. One problem with early studies using the think-aloud-protocol was that they used student translators. Using these subjects confused the real problems of translation with problems arising from inadequate language skills. Most studies now focus on the work of experienced translators (Krings 1986a, 1988).

The notion of translation process, which we shall take up in the next chapter, is of particular interest in the psycholinguistic and the practical models. In the practical model, the translation process is understood as *what the translator does* when he or she translates. Translation teachers and other scholars interested in the heuristics of translation have enumerated *translation strategies* which are distillations of the observation of practice. Such distillations, based on observable patterns of practice, have their cognitive counterparts. One goal of the psycholinguistic model should be to determine the cognitive substrates of observable patterns of practice. The cognitive substrates might then be matched with pedagogical concepts such as "translation strategy" to explain how transposition, modulation, equivalence and the other so-called translation strategies are psychologically realized.

It is unlikely that the intricate network of mental processes that make up translation can be neatly reduced to a series of heuristic translation methods such as amplification or transposition. Nevertheless, it might be possible to identify distinct categories of mental operations that take place in the working translator's mind. These operations would be combined in complex ways to produce specific linguistic patterns in target texts. Generalizations about textually realized patterns are the so-called "strategies" we teach to students in the classroom. Teachers are not the only ones who can benefit from psycholinguistic research. A better understanding of the psychology of translation can help those who work with the computational model. As software develops to the point where serious artificial intelligence is feasible, it might be possible for computers to learn from human translators. The cognitive strategies culled from think-aloud-protocols and from interviews might serve as templates for algorithms to control the inner workings of an intelligent translation machine.

The psycholinguist is interested in the cognitive effects of situational variables on the "internal" translation process. He or she is interested in the cognitive translation behaviors evoked in response to those variables. Some important research questions might include investigating the influence of language system, time constraints, levels of experience, information structure of the source text, and familiarity with the target culture on the cognitive processes of translation. Ultimately, the psycholinguistic model will find that the cognitive processes of translation are a unique subset of the cognitive strategies of text processing. They are related to text production and text comprehension. The psycholinguistic model can expose the intricate cognitive ways and means of translation as a textual process. The source text and the nascent target text are reference points at either end of the black box of translation.

Translation Theory: A Prologue

This summary of the models of translation is an attempt to explain some common factors and to resolve differences. Many controversies in translation studies might be quelled by a better understanding of how the different perspectives on translation relate to one another. Each model represents a particular point of view, but there are also significant interdependencies. Eventually, without yielding their specific perspectives, each of these models could contribute to a more ambitious and more adequate integrated theory of translation.

There is a great deal of confusion about what a theory of translation is and should be. Without dwelling in detail on the philosophical background of the notion of theory, it is clear that the expression is used by different scholars at different times for a variety of purposes. There is little attempt to distinguish the various senses of the term. There appears to be many levels of theory, each with different intersubjective authority. Some of the senses are mundane. To the layman, a theory is very much like an opinion. It is a common-sense construct which is descriptive and explanatory, but its intersubjective status is weak. Sometimes, by persuasion, or faith, or the use of compelling arguments, these opinion-like constructs are accepted by others. They achieve authority by consensus. These broadly-held opinions are sometimes called theories. Later, they may be codified into formal systems; the formalism adds rigor and the possibility of "proof" within the system. Sometimes a theory is an explanation derived by deduction or construction from such a system. The theories of literary criticism and linguistics are often of this type. Sometimes specific methods for uncovering patterns and verifying statements may be added to the system. The empirical theories of science are examples of theories augmented by verification methods. Given this confusing state of affairs, it is understandable that Newmark and others should deny the possibility of an integrated theory of translation (Newmark 1991).

This volume argues for an empirical approach. Alfred Schutz (1963, 235) characterizes the approach as involving "discovery through processes of controlled inference ... statable in propositional form and capable of being verified by anyone who is prepared to make the effort to do so through observation." Our call for an empirical approach to translation studies is not new. It is part of a general movement toward a more rigorous, observation-based and verifiable translation studies. It has been called for, among others, by Toury (1982) and Snell-Hornby (1988). Although she has not used the term "empirical," Snell-Hornby's agenda for an integrated translation studies dovetails in many respects with our own.

On what basis can it be claimed that an integrated theory is impossible? Is it because the subject of study is so complex? While complexity is an obstacle, to be sure, it is not a reason to deny an integrated theory. Translation scholars have already dealt with complexity by decomposing the problem. The models we have discussed each focus on one part of the larger issue. By fully developing each of these partial perspectives a holistic view might be constructed, but only if a common methodo-critical system is maintained. The notion of an integrated theory does not preclude special theories of scientific, literary, and poetic translation. This notion of diversity in integration is a central issue of Snell-Hornby's 1988 volume.

Our current conceptual disarray is a result of our motley genealogy. Proponents of the critical model use a variety of approaches, many derived from literary-critical and political "theory" systems (Lacan, Foucalt, Marx). Linguists and text-linguists often use formal systems derived from logical calculi and linguistics to express and validate their theories. Such theories are more like mathematical proofs. Psycholinguists of translation have adopted the empirical techniques of the behavioral scientists, and their theories are empirical. The pedagogues and translators using the practical model are interested in application theories. Such theories are based on the observation and recording of what appears to work. These, being observation based, are also empirical. It is, however, a naive empiricism. Sometimes pedagogues proceed simply from entirely subjective descriptions of "what has worked for them." These are first-order, not second-order formulations. What we accept as a theory depends on what we want from the theory, on the assumptions that we start with, and on the history and authority of the discourse which defines our profession. When these conditions are so different, then a common ground appears quite visionary.

Earlier we called for explicitness in translation studies. Scholars should reveal their research aims and research objectives. This explicitness should extend to the theoretical systems they use. If scholars say that their models are descriptive and explanatory, we need to know the bases on which this claim is made. Is the claim based on an elaborate argument, a critical apparatus, a closed conceptual system, a developed systematics, or the empirical method? An integrated empirical theory of translation which brings together the various perspectives is possible, but only within the limits of empiricism. Several integrated theories might be possible at once, each based on its own principles. What is not possible is integrating the motley mix which now characterizes translation studies. As long as the foundations of the common methods for the discipline are in doubt, an integrated theory is out of reach.

Having an integrated theory of translation does not presuppose that there will be one kind of translation proposed as the best kind of translation. The purpose of translation theory is not to propose that communicative or pragmatic translation is better than semantic or philological. This confuses the different types and techniques of translation with ways of describing and verifying our observations of translation. Different ways of doing translation, insofar as they actually occur, are the subject matter of translation studies, not its methods. We can accept, given our own arguments so far, that there are many different types of translation. The different forms arise from the fact that every translation is a dynamic intersection of translation situation with translation process. This intersection produces translation results which are always judged as texts. An integrated theory of translation should proceed from a focus on the description, explanation, and verification of statements about what is done, rather than what should be done, to produce target texts. Even here, the empirical approach may have a significant impact. Since the acceptability conditions for target texts may be assessed empirically, it could be possible to base translation heuristics on empirical results. Too often translation theorists work backwards from a particular style or type of translation, seeking to justify it. At this point in the development of our discipline we need to focus on the observable facts of translation and proceed forward to the generation of verifiable general statements.

Our observation of the facts of translation will probably show us that there is a virtual infinity of translation situations and a true infinity of translation results. The true stuff of translation studies is the body of translation practice, what translators actually do and how translation users react to what they do. Our task is to recognize in the infinite variety of the practice of translation significant patterns and regularities. We need to describe typical patterns, typical ways of dealing with problems, typical situations in which certain kinds of translation are preferred. It may be that there are no patterns in translation practice and each translation is completely unique, a kind of linguistic miracle. Then we would agree that translation theory is impossible. There can be no science of miracles. But, if we are allowed the single assumption that translation is not random, then an integrated empirical translation theory must be possible.

If we base translation theory on translation practice, then we are not faced with choosing linguistic/semantic over pragmatic/communicative approaches or emphasizing source-culture over target-culture values. Rather, we recognize that there is a translation reality which is extremely diverse and which calls for different translation responses. Our approach to translation insists that all of these approaches are valid if they have a basis in the textuality of translation and are empirical in method.

By basing translation theory on translation practice, we make an implicit argument for a translation studies which is based on the first-order phenomena of translation. The first-order facts of translation are centered on the text. They are actual source texts, actual textual situations, real first-order accounts of translation processes, and real reactions of readers to target texts. In the next chapters we shall address the specific textual factors that are the primary variables in an empirical approach to translation. At the end of this discussion we shall return to the issue of translation theory and summarize our agenda for a text-based empirical translation studies.

TWO

Translation: Knowledge and Process

LANGUAGE AS SYSTEM AND LANGUAGE IN USE

Translators use their ability to translate within specific interactional situations. Like speech and other uses of language, translation is always embedded in a communicative context. The practice of translation is a communicative activity that cannot be studied without accounting for the communicative context and its influence on the decision-making at the heart of the translation process.

Because of its genesis in linguistics and philology, there have always been two research directions in translation studies. These two directions are apparent in the models of translation we have discussed. One direction has emphasized the interactional and communicative features of translation as a form of language in use. The other has focused on the systemic nature of the linguistic relationships that exist in translation. For instance, the linguistic and the machine translation models are based on the systemic relations between source and target languages. The practical and text-linguistic models stress the performative and interactional aspects.

When we use language, when we are speaking, listening, writing, or reading, we are engaging in complex cognitive and communicative activities. These activities are systemic. Because they are regular and predictable, they can be described with rule-systems. They are said to be rule-governed. Reading, writing, speaking and hearing are also interactional because they involve communicating partners. Linguistic interaction takes place between individuals and between groups in a great, almost bewildering, variety of ways. Interpersonal face-to-face exchange is perhaps the most obvious mode of linguistic interaction, but it is certainly not the only one. There are many other means for acting and reacting using language. For instance, a person may "talk to himself" or deliver a monologue, presenting private thoughts to a listening audience. Much linguistic interaction occurs in real-time because the communicative partners are together in a common communicative situation. This immediacy is not always the case in linguistic interaction.

There are forms of linguistic interaction, such as broadcast journalism, which include speaking to and recording for an unseen audience. When we read great works of literature we are reading words that were placed on the page months or years before. Interaction may be delayed or displaced. Translation is an activity characterized by displacement. The communicating partners in translation are not temporally and physically co-present. Interaction is still possible because the communicating partners can always project one another's presence. The translator mediates between absent but projected authors and readers. The translator acts on their behalf, recoding the text "as if" all partners were present. The displacement of translation derives from its textuality. Written communication, delivered in the form of texts, is generally displaced. It is produced using a projection of the (future) reading audience. The communicative partnership is not completed in the presence of the producer, but later, after a time delay.

Human beings use language to reflect and communicate what they know and feel about physical and social reality. Everything human beings say, write, listen to, or read is the result of the twin processes of cognition and communication. Cognition cannot be separated from communication. They are a unified act rather than a sequence of two independent acts. Spoken discourse and written text are not neutral vessels filled by speakers and writers with language content. There is a complex relationship between cognitive content and communicative event, between knowledge and process. Discourses and texts always have communicative purpose and their linguistic expression reflects that purpose. The translator always acts with the interests of these twin processes in mind. Translators must account for the cognitive content of the communication, and they must use language in that accounting. The linguistic forms that are used must reflect the conditions governing the interaction. The term *situation* refers to the contextual constraints active during interaction. The competence of the translator is not just a knowledge of the two language systems, but also a communicative knowledge. Communicative knowledge is *knowing how to use language* in specific interactional situations. Translation competence is the sum total of what a translator needs to know, and needs to know how to do, in order to translate. Translation competence activates several cognitive domains in an integrated process.

The translator uses linguistic knowledge, and he or she uses communicative knowledge, a knowledge of the different interaction patterns in the two cultural communities. The translator also uses subject knowledge, a knowledge of the commercial, scientific, cultural and technical domains communicated through the text. Translation truly combines knowledge and communicative process.

Many traditional linguistic models ignore the communicative event. They concentrate on determining the regular distribution of grammatical and lexical forms. They detach these forms from the communicative events in which they were originally observed. This view of language assumes that there are context-free language structures. These structures are taken to be the primary objects of study. The utterances people actually experience in time and space are viewed as ephemeral surface phenomena which must be stripped of their contextual baggage. No real understanding of translation practice can be established using such a limited language-systemic approach.

The communicative and systemic views of language and translation seem mutually exclusive. A closer examination reveals that they are complementary. Language in use and language as system presuppose one another. Both approaches assume that human interaction is a patterned, rule-governed use of linguistic signs. The formal structures described by linguists are internalized through communicative interaction. Alternatively, the communicative events described by sociolinguists presume an underlying language system. The grammatical rules of the systemic linguist are formal representations of regularity. They describe what people seem to know about language. Without such regularities, language use would be impossible. Whatever justification there may be for the isolated study of linguistic interaction on the one hand, and the structural inventory and description of linguistic forms on the other, the complex study of language as a medium of human communication requires a synthesis of these two main strands of research.

The major research question of interactional linguistics is how to relate the network of social relations and actions to observable linguistic regularities. The translation scholar, who is also primarily interested in language interaction, has a similar question. How can he or she relate texts, the observable products of translation, to the significant textual variables, to translation situations, and to specific linguistic forms?

How can one arrive at a systematic description of language interaction using purely linguistic data? Individual linguistic elements, such as lexical items and grammatical structures, yield insufficient and unconnected bits of information about social interaction. As translators we cannot create, and as scholars we cannot predict, good translations by merely extrapolating target language structures using correspondence rules. Individual linguistic elements are, at best, indices to the interaction situation. Their value as pointers to cognitive processes and the communicative intentions of language users is limited.

It might be possible to overcome this difficulty by listing the linguistic markers that belong to typical interactional repertoires. These markers may be preferred by certain groups of language users; they may represent particular communicative strategies. They may reflect specific cognitive styles. Empirical sociolinguistic analysis has discovered a variety of distinct linguistic repertoires which function as indicators of interactional practice.

The sociolinguist's dilemma is that research along these lines yields, at best, a set of statistically based interactive potentials. Constructing polylectal grammars is much more difficult than building monolectal grammars (Bickerton 1973). Conflicting social norms would necessitate an intricate rule apparatus capable of describing *who* says *what*, *when*, *where*, *how* and to *whom*. Such polylectal grammars may eventually be written. At present, we "have only the vaguest notions as to what are the properties and structures of a polylectal grammar, and which of a number of possible forms it might best take" (Bickerton 1973, 18; Mitchell 1984).

The repertoires used in social interaction are examples of "variable-rule governed" linguistic communication in particular contexts. The contextualized manifestation of this rule-governed behavior is the *text*. It is variation in textual pattern that makes us aware of linguistic variation; thus, language in use is best studied in its textual manifestation (Labov 1970). Texts are the empirical basis for the study of structured interaction. If translation is a form of structured interaction between source text author, translator, and target text reader, then the text is also the communicative basis for the study of translation.

Classical grammatical theory abstracts structural information from the real contexts of communication. It typically reduces this information to linguistic units no larger than sentences. Furthermore, structural grammars usually assume ideal language users. Actual language use falls outside its scope of pertinence. The research goal of classical grammar is the description of an idealized competence. The objective is a grammatical knowledge potential uninfluenced by any kind of situational constraints. Linguistic competence is reduced to grammatical or formal competence.

Those who know a language also know how to use it. Full linguistic competence is not restricted to knowing the formal requirements for constructing grammatical sentences. It includes knowing how to use those sentences to build texts. Apart from the fact that individual utterances indicate the influence of performance constraints, there is also a fundamental strategic aspect that links sentences with texts. Sentences are used in the interest of texts. Sentence grammar must be seen as an integral component of a more encompassing text grammar. Text grammars, as models of textual knowledge, do more than extend our interest beyond the sentence; they lead to a basic reassessment of the structural categories that must be employed for the description and explanation of intra- and intersentential phenomena (Hartung 1981, 1307).[12]

Broadening the scope of grammatical theory to include textual data has unavoidably transformed the artificial research pattern of formal linguistics. It has motivated a more realistic study of the units of linguistic communication. The autonomy of the context-free grammar is challenged by the description of larger contextualized phenomena. Students of language are witnessing a paradigm shift. Old system-oriented models are being enhanced by communicative perspectives that take the text as their central frame of reference.

Translations as Interaction Structures

Texts are an appropriate starting point for the study of translation. Producing and receiving texts are activities that play a significant role in creating and maintaining social relations. This important role in social development is documented by the social diversity of textual exchange. A detailed analysis of the various textual modes of communication would be an excellent guide to the social networks they support. Texts are used as social tools. Like all tools, they reveal something about the tool-user.

As a natural consequence of our socialization in communities that share a diverse but fundamentally monolingual linguistic code, we have learned to produce and receive texts. These texts are patterned according to cultural conventions. Our social experience of texts does not give us the ability to master all of the textual conventions of our native language. Further, because knowledge of texts is a result of enculturation, the textual knowledge we have is culture-bound. This is a significant point for cross-cultural textual interchange. Because textual conventions are part of the larger linguistic code of a cultural community, they are *bound* to that community. This bond creates the "unnatural" aspect of translation we spoke about in the first chapter. Translation is an attempt to cross both linguistic and textual frontiers.

Translation is motivated by a common desire to cross that frontier. The source language (henceforth L_1) user and the target language (henceforth L_2) user want to communicate with one another. To accomplish this they ask translators to take *source texts*, which in the overwhelming majority of cases (interpreting excepted) have already fulfilled their communicative purposes, and recreate them as members of the *text world* of the target language. A text world is the repertoire of textual interaction structures used in a particular communicative community.

The source text, as an instance of social activity, has already completed its communicative function. The production and reception of the untranslated source text within its normal cultural context is usually problem-free. The smooth flow of communication is a function of the directedness of the texts within the L_1 community. Many specialized texts have specific audiences. They reflect the unique expertise of specific authors, and they reflect special purposes in their textual organization. The structure of each text is a specific interactional structure which has evolved, or been created, to carry out particular interactional aims. Scientific texts, legal documents, commercial transactions, and technical manuals are typical examples of specialized texts. They exhibit a high degree of directedness as a result of the shared special interests and mutual knowledge that exist between particular groups of senders and receivers. There is no clear-cut dividing line between specialized texts and the more general texts that facilitate the great bulk of intracultural communication. The textual world of a culture is not homogeneous. Textual knowledge is not evenly distributed. Communicators do not have access to all of the textual forms available for use. They do not have a social need to use them. Within the society as a whole many texts are used only by particular communicating sub-groups.

The translator must assess the transformations which should be made to the L_1 text in order to meet the conditions of need and expectation required by the L_2 audience. These transformations are not just linguistic transformations. Translations, like their source language progenitors, are manifestations of social interaction. Like normal texts, they must exhibit social directedness. The naturalness of a text in its cultural context is a function of how closely it correlates with the expectations that come from the audience's pragmatic experience with similarly situated and directed texts. Audiences have a *common sense knowledge* of texts that takes the form of a naive typology of texts. This first-order categorization is often unexpressed and is rarely described systematically.[13] Texts are part of the familiar scenes of everyday life and are seen as "perceivedly normal courses-of-action" that "everybody knows" (Schutz 1970). These taken-for-granted constructs have been likened to recipes (Schutz 1970, 81):

> The recipe works, on the one hand, as a precept for actions, and thus serves as a scheme of expression: whoever wants to obtain a certain result has to proceed as indicated by the recipe provided for this purpose. On the other hand, the recipe serves as a scheme of interpretation; whoever proceeds as indicated by a specific recipe is supposed to intend the correlated result. If a translation is to succeed it must follow the recipe for textual communication in the target culture. If it does not, it cannot function as a scheme of interpretation for the text user.

Texts create interest, in the widest sense of the word, primarily by their information content and not by their textual appearance. The target community is interested in what the texts contain. It is, however, a text's adherence to the textual conventions of the cultural community that allows a text consumer to receive the contents of the text without being misled by the package it has arrived in. Adherence to textual convention imparts a characteristic *textual profile* to the text. A textual profile is the set of features, including arrangements of linguistic markers, that allows a user to identify the recipe that is being used. Most of the time a text user is not consciously aware of textual profiles and the set of expectations that he or she brings to a text. These expectations emerge into consciousness only in their violation. When a user says that a translation "doesn't sound right," it is a recognition of textual expectations that have been violated.

Translations have to compete within the communicative environment of the L_2. All normal (untranslated) texts in the L_2 are the natural result of L_2 communicative situations. They conform to the textual norms and traditions of their users. Translations "straddle" the two language communities. They project communicative activities from one interaction locus to another. They are, as we have said, displaced interaction structures. A text written for the reader of the source language is transformed to satisfy the information needs of an audience for which it was not originally intended. A need for the information in the L_1 text is assumed. Without this need, translation is not required. Translations are valuable to L_2 audiences because they offer information that would not otherwise be available in the L_2

community. A translation's success in meeting this need is not just a function of the user's desire for the information. Success is also dependent on the user's ability to receive and process the information encoded in the text.

The typical reader is not consciously aware of the formal requirements of the text that he or she reads. Text consumers recognize the naturalness of a text in a naive way. The translator, on the other hand, must understand the text more explicitly. The translator must not only know about the contrastive linguistics of the language pair, but must also know about contrastive textual requirements. Translators must have a conscious appreciation of the textual structure of the target text. This is quite difficult if the target language is not their native language.

The translator's knowledge of the text is like the second-order knowledge of the translation scholar. It must be constructed deliberately and methodically. Translation competence, knowing how to translate, is a constructed competence. It is built through directed experience and conscious reflection. It is a conjunction of knowledge about multiple languages with knowledge about multiple textual systems.

Translation as Process

The frame of reference created by the concepts of interaction and text allows the translation theorist to look beyond sentence boundaries to describe more global structures. Using the idea that a text is an interaction structure identifies translation studies as a linguistic and social science. Translation cannot deny its social character by claiming that it is an art. Referring to translation as an art does not fundamentally alter its status as a cross-cultural, cross-linguistic, text-producing activity. The translation process is one of text-induced text production. Translation results are, uniquely, *text-induced texts*.

Translation process and translation result are integrally related. The processual aspect will be treated first primarily for methodological reasons. Earlier we introduced the idea of translation competence. Now we must describe how translation competence is activated. Translation process is the activation of competence in a translation situation. The result of the translation process is a target text. Thus, translation is a kind of text production. Text linguistics, among other disciplines, is currently developing theories that explain text production processes. It is within the evolving framework of a science of text production and text comprehension that translation process has to be studied. It is not surprising that the study of translation calls for research objectives that stretch the current boundaries of linguistics. Even the interactionist perspective of the sociolinguist emphasizes the forms of speech interaction instead of the processes. We need more than a comprehensive inventory of textual or interactional structures to understand translation. In order to understand translation activities (*translatorische Tätigkeiten*), we need to broaden our scope to include an account of how those structures are produced and understood. The first serious attempts to categorize translation problems were influenced by an awareness of the systemic differences between L_1 and L_2. A systematic description of the two languages was seen as a prerequisite for a comparison of elements and structures based on their matching potential in translation. Translation was thought to rely on regular relations or correspondences between the constituent levels of the L_1 and the L_2. Lexical items of the L_1 were supposed to be partially or completely replaceable by lexical items of the L_2. Likewise, L_1 grammatical structures had their counterparts in the L_2. Actually, exact correspondences between discrete lexical or grammatical elements are relatively rare. In translation practice, L_1-L_2 pairings usually turn out to be pairings of lexical-grammatical complexes. Lexical resources are used when grammatical mechanisms fail, and more rarely, L_2 grammatical structures are used to replace L_1 lexical distinctions.

This view of translation correspondences was fundamentally mechanical. Translation was no more than the replacement of components of one system, the L_1, by components of another system, the L_2. A natural corollary of this approach, which characterized translation theory in the sixties (Catford 1965; Neubert 1968), was the belief that translation studies was primarily a linguistic endeavor. Admittedly, it was a linguistics which had adopted an explicitly functional perspective, where a complex language system interacted with the constraints and conditions of real communication events. Even so, the processes of human communication were seen as acting primarily on the linguistic system and were therefore linguistic processes (Catford 1965, 1).[14]

A decisive step was made in the seventies by a number of linguists and translation theorists when language functions were reinterpreted as textual functions. Language processes were attached to textual processes and language processing was expanded to include *text processing*. Authors, translators, and readers process more than words and grammatical structures. They engage in a more encompassing information processing activity which includes the processing of words and grammatical structures. This higher level of processing includes the synthesis of meaning structures, the factoring of pragmatic constraints, and the global conditioning of the linguistic surface of the text. Linguistic system, pragmatic constraints, world knowledge, and meaning systems all converge in the act of translation. Translation is a synthetic process in which the translator dynamically matches semantic, syntactic, textual, and pragmatic fields to create a unitary whole, the L_2 text.

How can this complex activity be decomposed into more manageable units of analysis? The processing of texts presupposes a processing competence. It may be possible to decompose processing competence into smaller, more conceptually manageable units. According to Eikmeyer (1983, 12), "the assumption is that underlying every process there is a procedure ... which, when executed, manifests the process token. ... Processes are entities which are embedded into the flow of time. They have a starting point, they run for a span of time and end up with a result. Processes emerge from the execution of other kinds of entities which I will call procedures."

Procedures may be one constituent of translation and text processing competence. The procedural knowledge of a translator can be seen as the composite of all the things a translator knows how to do, either consciously or unconsciously, when translating. Procedural knowledge includes knowledge about using language and knowledge about using texts. Much of this procedural knowledge has been acquired through experience. The ability to use texts is a general text processing ability the translator shares with other members of society. However, some procedural knowledge, especially in the case of translation, has been acquired by special experience and training. As we experience texts, our text processing ability is enhanced, giving us the ability to produce texts of our own. Each text that we produce and interpret is part of a continuing progression of texts, a textual stream, from which we build our competence. Each new text that we encounter or create is processed using knowledge that has been accumulated via the processing of countless earlier texts.

All functioning members of human society have some common text processing ability, a general textual competence. It should be stressed, however, that human beings know when, where, and how to process a wide variety of different kinds of texts. Active and passive experience with texts in a myriad of different settings constructs a context-sensitive textual competence.[15] Specific texts can be produced for specific situations.

The textual competence of the speaker exists in conjunction with his or her linguistic competence. Linguistic competence, the ability to produce those and only those sentences "allowed" in the language, is only observable as an expression of textual (discursive) competence. Knowledge of texts and textual procedures enables the communicator to process the language in texts. The knowledge allows the communicator to produce, understand, and, if necessary, to translate, supra-sentential linguistic structures. These structures are more than mere concatenations of morphemes and sentences. A text is more than a "super-sentence."[16]

The process-oriented view of translation poses a number of difficult research questions. How do translators activate their textual knowledge during communication? How are ideas placed in texts, and how do listeners and readers receive the texts and recover the ideas they convey? Furthermore, how do pragmatic constraints affect the linguistic and semantic profile of the text? In order to be effective, a translator has to tap into both the L_1 and L_2 textual competences. A translator must understand what the L_1 text is doing and what information it contains before he can recreate it for an L_2 audience. The translator's text processing knowledge must include both L_1 procedural knowledge and L_2 procedural knowledge. Further, even though the translator's competence is based on a general text processing competence distributed in the culture, there are procedural components which are not part of general textual competence.

All texts are embedded in space and time; they are delivered by someone, to someone. They are the result of a process with a beginning and an end. While we may conceive of a textual competence as composed of an inventory of textual procedures, it is these procedures, evoked and applied in real-time, that manifest the textual process. For the purposes of analysis we can group textual procedures around two poles: production and reception. The production pole is a cover term for various overlapping sub-processes (Meyer 1975):

1. First, the text producer has a plan to communicate some information content.[17] This planning stage already assumes a certain textual profile. It involves a single choice from a larger number of options. It may also center on certain attitudinal states, such as informing, questioning, ordering, persuading, entertaining, or defending.

2. Following the inception phase is an ideational phase which gives substance to the planning initiative. This phase involves the development of a configuration of ideas to be communicated us-

ing the text plan. This semantic stage does not appear *sui generis*, but is incipient in the planning stage.

3. The configuration of ideas is developed as the result of a plan. This development stage is well along in the textual process. Ideas are increasingly verbalized and move closer to the surface. Development is effected by apportioning communicative values among the components of the overall ideational configuration. It specifies and summarizes, expands and condenses, rearranges, and orders a previously less structured complex. Most importantly, development involves creating interconnectedness within the idea complex, using techniques such as introducing, progressing, and finalizing. Development imparts a definite contour or shape to the set of ideas the communicator intends to communicate. There is no doubt that development is channeled by pragmatic parameters, but the broad character of the ideational sequence will reflect the text-typical sequencing associated with choices made in the planning phase.

4. The ideational sequence is given concrete verbal expression. The expression stage is the necessary concretization of the textual process, but it is also a point of no return. However ambitious the plan, however rich the ideation and multifaceted the development, once the expression stage is reached, the productive textual process is brought to an end. Constrained by the selections made in the preceding stages, the text producer chooses expressions that seem to fit most adequately into the pattern of plan, ideation, and development.

5. Finally, concrete verbal expressions are given their final surface representations. This last phase is sometimes referred to as *parsing*, indicating that the "conventional" surface text has been reached. The verbal expressions of the previous stage, still mental constructs, now succumb to the constraints of grammar and lexis.

The five phases of planning, ideation, development, expression, and parsing should not be considered distinct linear stages. They represent the gross progression and natural order of text production, but there may be movement backwards and forwards; there is a constant cycling between the phases. Decisions are continually revised. For instance, parsing may fail on a chosen expression and a new one must be chosen. Choosing a particular expression at the expressive phase could trigger further expansion within the development phase.

Face-to-face communication, with its immediate give and take, will have a greater impact on the progression of planning, ideation, and development than less dynamic forms of communication such as public speaking. Nevertheless, while there is bound to be typological variation in the way texts are produced, and differences in the amount of cycling between the stages of production, it is clear that the general process of text production is not linear.

Text production is, of course, only one part of textual interaction. Texts are produced to be interpreted. In most cases their sole purpose is to be understood. A person who receives a text has the surface text as a starting point. By parsing surface expressions, he or she is able to determine their functional load. The linear order of the text and grammatical dependencies are used to identify the concepts conveyed by expressions. The arrangement of the concepts behind the expressions points to a more global arrangement. This leads to the recovery of the main ideas of the text. The recovery of the ideational sequence(s) brings the receiver-interpreter to an appreciation of the text producer's intended plan.

Although text comprehension shares certain features with text production, it should be noted that the text comprehender does not simply reverse the progression of textual processing. Understanding is a distinct process. Text production is principally a message-constructing process where meanings, ordered and developed according to an underlying plan, are attached to linguistic signs. In text comprehension, the receiver builds up a model of what the linguistic signs are supposed to mean. The distinction, simply put, is one of meaning first (production) and meaning last (understanding). It is not a distinction between active sender and passive receiver; both are active participants in the textual process. One of the key findings of modern cognitive psychology is that text comprehension only occurs when the comprehender actively conjectures or projects the semantic content contained in the text (Miller 1983). Understanding requires the creation, testing, and rejection or validation of hypotheses about the meaning of the text being received. Text comprehension is assisted when the text has been constructed in such a way that the reader is guided to project semantic content. Providing such assistance is a major responsibility of the translator.

The comprehension process begins when the first sentence of a text is received. The subject matches stored knowledge with the extracted semantic content of the incoming text. Messages of interest contain new information the receiver wants to know. The new information is delivered in known formats, using the familiar vehicles of a common language and expected textual profiles. If everything were new, understanding would break down. Sender and receiver have to share a common procedural inventory to ensure that the information embedded in the "sent" text matches the information retrieved from the "received" text. There is a common textual framework presupposed by both comprehender and producer. This framework is a set of procedural attachments that ensures a pattern-matching potential between the text as an output of the sender and the same text as an input for the receiver (Winograd 1975, 203–208; Bobrow and Winograd 1977).

The translator provides a channel between one set of procedural attachments and another. The translator converts one set of codes and structures to a second set by applying translation procedures to the L_1 text. The procedural attachments include mechanisms for:

1. Decoding the surface structure of the L_1 text

2. Retrieving the ideational content of the L_1 text from the surface expression

3. Identifying the plan and development of the L_1 text from the ideational configuration

4. Restructuring the expression, development, and plan of the text according to L_2 standards

5. Encoding the modified expression, development, and plan in L_2 linguistic structures

The translation process can be seen as a special case of the text production–text comprehension activity cycle. The translator intervenes in the cycle, embedding a second text comprehension–text production pair within a first. This embedding is characteristic of translation as a form of intercultural communication.

We have called translation a process, but what are the details of this process? We have said that the translation process has constituent elements (steps, operations, subprocesses, procedures), and the application of these constituent operations to textual representations over time produces a target text. Some of the constituent operations of the overall process belong to an inventory of general text processing procedures. For instance, when a translator reads a source text before translating it, this reading ability and the ability to construct an understanding of the text are based on general text processing capacities. Reading for translation, like reading for paraphrasing, reflects a dependence on general text comprehension processes. This common substrate does not mean that the general processes are unaffected by the specific task. Reading for translation may resemble reading for paraphrase and reading for understanding, but it differs in certain task-related ways (Shreve, Danks, Schäffner, and Griffin n.d.).

A program for the analysis of process in translation should focus on determining:

1. How general text processing activities (reading, comprehension, writing) are conditioned or altered by the influence of the translation task

2. If there are translation-specific procedures which do not appear (or appear rarely) in normal text-processing (e.g., transposition)

3. The relationship of text processing and its component procedures to other cognitive processes and procedures (memory, perception, problem-solving)

4. The declarative knowledge required as inputs to translation procedures

5. The general configuration and progression of operations or procedures in the overall translation process

6. The empirical relationship between cognitive procedures, target texts, the translator's own understandings of the translation process, and heuristic expressions of the translation process

The program is based on the premise that translators use both general text processing procedures and translation-specific procedures. It also assumes that text processing occurs in combination with other cognitive processes and cannot be separated from them. The last two items in the program are perhaps the most important. We assume that a simple inventory of procedures is not enough to explain the translation process. We must understand how the mental operations act upon and influence one another as they are applied. It is clear that these procedures are not part of a simple sequential process; they are not activated in a fixed order. Their temporal and sequential relationships are more complex. The entire convoluted process resembles a network more than a chain. Procedures from several cognitive domains are probably active simultaneously. The progression of text comprehension and text production procedures is probably guided by problem-solving procedures, assisted by information recall, storage, and integration procedures, and monitored by pattern-matching and planning procedures. There can be no clear prediction of which procedures will be activated or what sequence they will be activated in. Multiple factors influence the course of any individual act of translation. It is not our place here to specify the cognitive aspects of the translation process. That determination must be the result of empirical study carried out by the psycholinguists of translation.

Our program also raises the issue of procedural hierarchy. Any analysis of translation process must explain the relationships between:

1. The cognitive level of translation process and procedure
2. The textual level of translation process and procedure
3. The first-order descriptive level of translation process and procedure
4. The second-order descriptive level of translation process and procedure

The cognitive level deals with accessing the "black box" of the psycholinguistic model. The procedures at this level are mental operations, only some of which are conscious. It is important to understand that psycholinguistic methods such as the think-aloud-protocol, while important, only provide evidence of cognitive operations that are conscious.

At the textual level we have target texts, the manifest results of the operation of cognitive procedures. These procedural outputs must be correlated with the cognitive activities that produced them. The relationships between textual results and cognitive procedures are probably not simple one-to-one relationships. A sentence in the target text may be the textual result of several procedures applied in a specific sequence.

At the first-order descriptive level, we have the reflections and reactions of translators and translation users to textual results (or their reactions, as in think-aloud-protocols, to the conscious manifestations of the translation process). These first-order descriptions of procedures represent the translator's own accounts of what he or she has done (or is doing). Of necessity, the translator's own accounting is a typification and generalization. Translators cannot describe in detail all of the mental operations they carry out. Active reflection on experience will identify as a coherent course-of-action only *conscious* manifestations of a more complex underlying process. This course-of-action is a kind of projection or plan based on the regularity of past experience. Even if translators do not verbally reflect on the translation process for a listening psycholinguist, they still engage in a cognitive reflection that consolidates and represents the complex activity they perform. Were this not the case, there would be no pattern in the approaches a translator takes to successive translations. A translator does not exhibit random behavior with respect to the translation task; he or she does not react in simple response. The translator knows, in a general way, what has to be done to translate the text. The translator's knowledge is based on successes and failures with previous texts. As the translator moves through the text, certain textual configurations trigger recognitions. The recognitions invoke preexistent internalized courses-of-action. These conscious acts and decisions are supported by unconscious mental operations. The translator adopts particular approaches and consciously utilizes particular combinations of procedures. The translator is aware, in advance, of what can be done to the text. A translator knows how to translate at the first-order level. The translator knows how to achieve particular textual results, even if he or she doesn't know all of the constituent mental operations that support translation performance. These learned and internalized mental operations are at a lower procedural level and are triggered by the translator's deliberate movement through the text.

At the second-order descriptive level, we have the hypotheses and generalizations of the translation theorist. The second-order level involves generalization about typical courses-of-action exhibited by translators. The theoretical constructs developed at this level are also typifications. They generalize about the recurrent features of translation practice. Some translation theorists have talked about translation "procedures" and translation "strategies." Indeed, these are useful concepts. But at what level of our four-tier model of process are these procedures? For example, Gerardo Vázquez-Ayora compiled an impressive list of strategies in his *Introducción a la Traductología:*

1. transposition

2. modulation

3. equivalence

4. adaptation

5. amplification

6. explicitation

7. omission

8. compensation

Other students of translation have compiled similar lists. The status of these "strategies" must be clarified. They are second-order typifications. They have been condensed from the observation of practice and are an expression of regularity. They are not cognitive procedures, although they are reflections of the results of cognitive procedures. They are not the translator's own first-order courses-of-action, but they are expressions of the results of those courses-of-action.

When we use the words process and procedure, we don't always distinguish which of these levels we are referring to. Just as there are many "translations," there are many translation processes. There is translation process considered as a complex set of mental operations in a cognitive network. There is translation process considered as a pattern of procedural outputs. There is translation process considered as typical courses-of-action applied by practicing translators to actual texts. There is translation process considered as theoretical construct, describing and accounting for the regularities observed in translation practice. These second-order constructs may find their way, as they should, into the translation classroom where they may be offered as heuristics, even prescriptions, for good translation practice.

Knowledge and Mutual Knowledge

Procedures are a form of knowledge. They are condensations of experience which emerge as typical mental or physical courses-of-action used by actors to achieve results in the world of everyday life. Procedures are not just about doing things; they are also about knowing things and knowing what to do with things. Any consideration of translation process and procedure must deal with what translators and other text processors must know in order to produce and understand texts. If translations are outputs of textual processes, what are the inputs? The answers to this question are: knowledge of language, knowledge of social interaction, knowledge of the world (and its domains), knowledge of texts, and knowledge of translation. Over the course of the next several pages, we will address issues of knowledge organization which relate to the translator's ability to process texts.

Much recent text processing research has centered on the concept of *mutual knowledge*. The concept includes the procedural knowledge (knowing how to do things) and declarative knowledge (knowing about things) necessary for text processing (Smith 1982; Clark and Marshall 1981). Mutual knowledge is knowledge that is shared and known to be shared (Smith 1982, xii). It is the result of common experience. Originally introduced by Lewis (1969, 25–27) as "mutual confidence," the concept has since been referred to as conversational context, common ground, common act of presumption, shared set contextual domain, tacit assumptions, pragmatic presupposition, normal beliefs, mutual beliefs, and shared knowledge.

Common to all of these formulations is the premise that communication succeeds because participants share a body of common experience. Portions of this experience are activated by the texts they exchange. Mutual knowledge is based on a history of action in a common cultural and social background. Mutual knowledge is possible because partners meet a fundamental requirement for text comprehension, community membership (Clark and Marshall 1981, 37).

Mutual knowledge is clearly a fundamental translation issue. The translator must act as a bridge between the knowledge of one cultural group and the knowledge of another. Without the translator there is a knowledge gap. The knowledge gap involves more than knowledge of production and comprehension procedures. It also involves knowledge of cultural values and mores, of economic and social structures, and of terminological and legal systems. The translator transfers more than a linguistic package when a text is translated. The contents are also transferred. Translators must act as *knowledge brokers* between the members of two disjunct communities. A fundamental task for the translator is determining what the L_2 text recipient knows and deciding what the translation should provide in compensation for what the L_2 text recipient does not know. An important element of the translation process must be an ability to account for the knowledge differential between communities. This implies that some translation procedures need to function as compensation mechanisms. Compensation can occur in different ways. To compensate for linguistic difference (the partners don't know one another's languages) the translator uses his or her knowledge of both languages to recreate the text in the target language. To compensate for a lack of cultural knowledge (for example, the meaning of a cultural allusion in a source text) the translator might decide to add explanatory information to the target text. In the first case, the translator compensates for lack of mutual knowledge by re-processing the text linguistically and textually. In the second case, the translator performs a primarily semantic operation by expanding the referential scope of the target. To compensate for lack of mutual knowledge, the translator has to be aware of the scope of the knowledge differential. The translator has to know what the target community does and does not know.

Community can refer to social relations at a variety of levels. The term does not imply the broadest level of possession of a common culture. A less vague, but still very broad, distinction can be made by referring to all speakers of English or German or Russian. While it is true that membership in a speech community is an important factor, equating community with speech community is too general. What is required is a definition of membership which reflects the range of communicative interaction and the systematic variety of texts accepted in a society. Within a speech community, there are a heterogeneous range of speakers and a broad inventory of texts connected to socially defined political, legal, vocational, cultural, moral, and religious contexts. The translator has to know the linguistic and textual abilities of the target community and he or she has to assess the knowledge resources brought to the translation.

Mutual knowledge means that a communicating partner is able to *know that the other knows too*. The social distribution of knowledge in the community allows communicators to presume a shared inventory of textual and linguistic conventions if a mutual knowledge of community membership is established. Clark and Marshall (1981, 37) have spoken of the presumption of *community co-membership*. This presumption is active when a scientist writes a report for colleagues in the same field; when a teacher talks to his class; when parents converse with their children; when a doctor communicates with his patients; when husband and wife exchange words of mutual trust or intimacy. Because translators act in the place of original authors of texts, they must also make assumptions of co-membership. They must act "as if" they were members of the target community.

Mutual knowledge and community membership are socially based concepts. Specific communicative conditions arise when communication occurs in socially defined contexts. There specific conditions that obtain when partners playing social roles like parent, child, husband, and wife meet to exchange information. The communicative community that is presumed during an act of communication is a dynamic presumption, made in the duration of the communicating act, and dropped for another when necessity arises. Co-membership is like social role in this respect. Some of our roles are long-term; others are transitory. Presumptions of community co-membership and mutual knowledge are activated and exist only during the life of the communicative event. Most translators, unless they have specialized in particular kinds of texts addressed to specific groups, constantly assume a variety of communicative roles. Imagine, if you will, the translator asked to translate a love letter for a partner in an inter-linguistic romance. Can the translator fulfill the commission without identifying in some way with the partners in this interaction?

During communication there is a tacit understanding that a particular domain of mutual knowledge is called for, one which includes role relations. There is a selection of textual procedures from a broader inventory and a selection of knowledge elements from a wider set. Communicators adjust their textual activity; they constrain the processing which occurs. Each partner makes assumptions about the textual activity which is about to occur. This common assumption has been called a universality of knowledge. It is a very limited universality; it is no more than the shared presumptions of communicating partners playing socially conditioned communicative roles in particular contexts. Co-members take the contents of their mutual knowledge for granted. The contents are assumed to be present but are not invested with a particular value. Their truth value may be irrelevant. What is important is that knowledge is shared and presumed to be shared.

Copresence

Presumptions of mutual knowledge are based on *copresence*. Copresence may be thought of as the logical grounds for presuming mutual knowledge of objects, events, things, people, and places (Clark and Marshall 1981, 38–39; Sperber and Wilson 1982, 64–65). Presumption may be based on *immediate copresence*. For example, A and B talk to one another about C; C is a person, object, or event experienced in physical proximity. If A and B know, however, that they have both experienced (seen, heard, smelled, tasted, touched, felt) C before, then they may rely on *prior physical copresence* instead. This kind of copresence is based on the ability to recall and applies to most topics treated in written communication and translation. Prior physical copresence is also the situation where B is not in face-to-face interaction with A, but A has met B before, as in the case where A is writing a letter to B. There are cases where interactants are not in contact and have never been in contact. They have not had a common physical experience of the things to which their communication refers. There are cases where objects and events are projected from experience; they are imagined. This is *potential physical copresence*. Our actual physical experience of objects, events, states, and processes is infinitesimal, relative to the physical contacts we might have made. Potential physical copresence allows for the rational projection of objects and phenomena and provides a basis for presuming mutual knowledge.

Linguistic copresence creates realms of mutual knowledge that, although based on concrete experience, may never have been concrete. Language allows us to create worlds of the most diverse kinds where writers and readers or speakers and hearers may be copresent. These are virtual, as opposed to actual experiences. Many things which are referred to in texts, and which become a part of our mutual knowledge, have an existence only as references of texts. These objects, events, or persons are referred to as if they had been encountered in objective reality. They are referred to in the same way as things with which we are physically copresent. Thus, we can refer to devils, witches, unicorns, and fairies in much same way that we refer to chairs and tables and mushrooms.

There are limitations. All forms of copresence are constrained. Partners in communication are not at liberty to coin new words and insert them in completely unexpected textual constructions if they expect to be understood. A precondition of linguistic copresence is the axiom of *understandability*. This is a complex assumption which entails that partners in communication mutually index the events, objects, items, and individuals mentioned in their discourse to the same loci in their respective (internalized) language systems. This allows the objects to assume a mutually shared meaning. The translator must be concerned with copresence because he or she is concerned with understandability. The form of copresence underlying the presumption of mutual knowledge has a direct bearing on the way the translator renders the target text. If the translator is aware that there are two communicating groups, each member of which is personally and physically familiar with the objects and events referenced in the text, then the language use in the text may be quite telegraphic. Scientific and technical translators often get away with a great economy of language because the partners for whom they are translating have strong grounds of prior physical copresence for presuming mutual knowledge. German automotive technicians reading an American automotive repair manual have, on the whole, seen the same objects, used the same tools, participated in the same installations and assemblies, and made the same repairs. The knowledge differential is smaller and a translation of the repair manual would have to compensate very little. A translator in this situation could use fewer explicitations than if he or she were translating for an audience, not of auto repairmen, but Saturday morning mechanics like the authors.

Linguistic copresence has prior and potential forms. In prior linguistic copresence items are referred to by one partner that were heard or read by the other partner before, either in the same text or in his or her previous linguistic experience.[18] The basis for prior linguistic copresence is the recallability of items and their references. Potential linguistic copresence is involved when a partner in the process of communication replaces a linguistic reference with other linguistic items which can function as potential equivalents. Examples include pronouns, synonyms, hyponyms, superordinate terms, metaphors, metonyms, and so on. All of these items establish potential linguistic copresence. They are (it might be said) analogous to potential physical copresence because they are locatable as coreferential items in the communicative process. This form of copresence assumes an important role in establishing cohesion, a textual characteristic we shall discuss in some detail in the next chapter.

Copresence may be direct or indirect. As an example, if one person shows another a picture he had bought and says *The price was ten dollars*, the other person can infer from the physically present picture that the amount refers to its indirectly copresent price. On this basis he can establish mutual knowledge of its identity. The inference is based upon socially distributed knowledge about prices and objects. Objects, like paintings, have an association with prices; it is knowledge of the association that establishes *indirect* copresence. In the sentence, *I've done the pools for several years but I've never won a penny*, communication succeeds because the partners in the communication have a mutual knowledge based on their membership in the British community. They understand that in the pools one can win money. The item *pools* and the item *money* are only indirectly related in the text; copresence is established by associativity.

Indirect linguistic copresence is of enormous importance in communication. The intelligibility of connected discourse depends on the breadth of mutual knowledge and is continually expanded by the creation of associative ties between items in the sequential flow of the text. Texts are carriers of information; this means that they contain new information embedded in a matrix of old and previously shared information. References to new items, objects, events, states, and processes can be comprehended because they may be logically related through indirect linguistic copresence to other already understood items. The translator has to understand these relationships because they imply that the lexical and grammatical choices made for the target text cannot be random. The references indexed by the linguistic choices must reflect the associative relationships indexed by the corresponding source text words and phrases. They have to be chosen because they establish, as a whole, the same associativity. Perfect identity is not possible. The target associative network can never be identical to that of the source. Identity is precluded by the fact that the conceptual referents of lexical items in language pairs do not always coincide. The translator, nevertheless, strives for an equivalence of effect and communicative value.

In the sentence, *I've done the pools for several years, but I can't remember having had to wait for half an hour,* the ability to associate *doing the pools* with *having had to wait* is weaker than the ability to associate *playing the pools* and *winning money.* There is a high degree of linkage in the first case and a lesser degree in the second case. If the utterance were to continue with, *and I've gambled on horses,* the associative tie would be very weak. There is only a weak association between betting the pools and betting on horses. Nevertheless, all of these are cases of indirect linguistic copresence (Clark and Marshall 1981, 41). Readers take all associable textual elements into consideration; they draw conclusions from the patterns they form. In everyday speech, physical copresence is most often used to establish mutual knowledge. In the case of written communication, indirect linguistic copresence is the most common basis for mutual knowledge. Mutual knowledge and indirect linguistic copresence are critical factors in text-processing and translation. Although indirect linguistic copresence is ultimately founded in physical experience, it has acquired an independence that makes it particularly suited as a guarantor of text comprehension. It enables text producer, translator, and text comprehender to communicate with one another as if the text were a perfect model of the physical and social world. The text constitutes a *possible world* that functions as a substitute for objective reality. It is on the strength of the projective power of the textual process that senders and receivers are able to activate one another's mutual knowledge.

Frames

Text comprehension is dependent on a mutual knowledge that is most frequently established through indirect linguistic copresence. How is it that texts manage to use linguistic copresence as an information carrier between sender and receiver? How does one partner in the communicative event construct language so that it is textually productive? How can connected segments and chunks of semantic and pragmatic information be transmitted in the form of associative networks of linguistic references to items of mutual knowledge? How does the other partner interpret the textually embedded network so that it gives access to the knowledge world constituted by the network?

The process in question is an *actualizing* of language in texts by selecting options from the linguistic system. The author of a source text has already selected options from the L_1 system. New options must be selected by the translator from the L_2 system using the associative framework embedded in the L_1 text as a guideline. The progressions and structures that established mutual knowledge and intelligibility in the L_1 must be re-established in the target language. The translator is really translating textually realized associative structures, not words. The translator must replace the foundation for mutual knowledge that was removed when L_1 text and L_2 audience were paired.

If languages are virtual systems, then texts are *actual* systems. They are actual because they involve real choices that text producers and translators must make from the linguistic repertoire to activate elements of the knowledge repertoire. The knowledge repertoires from which producers and comprehenders make their choices are not random repositories of linguistic and world knowledge. They are highly structured. The concepts of mutual knowledge and associative network presume an underlying body of socially distributed and organized linguistic, social, and textual knowledge. Community co-members, as a result of their common enculturation, organize their experience in ways that support the establishment of mutual knowledge through linguistic copresence. This organization of experience may be referred to as *framing* and the knowledge structures themselves as *frames*.

Frames are the fabric from which texts are woven. They are not prefabricated potential texts; they are building blocks from which texts are assembled. Fillmore presents a cogent rationale for the frame concept when he says: "we must add to the description of grammar and lexicon a description of the cognitive and interactional 'frames' in terms of which the language user interprets his environment, formulates his own messages, understands the messages of others, and accumulates or creates an internal model of his world" (Fillmore 1976, 23).

Cognitive frames resemble semantic fields. They group together semantic quanta belonging to larger semantic domains. Fillmore's own example of a cognitive frame is the one containing the words for commercial event: terms such as *buy, sell, pay, cost, spend,* or *charge*. Any one of these English words is capable of accessing the entire frame. Access may be effected by any one of these words, but each item highlights or foregrounds only one small section of the frame (Fillmore 1976, 25). The *commercial event frame* is the same in German as it is in English: *kaufen, verkaufen, bezahlen, kosten, ausgeben,* and *verlangen*. Speakers of the two languages evidently organize their buying and selling experiences in much the same way. From a linguistic point of view, they access this cognitive frame in a similar fashion. Lexical items point to congruent regions of generally isomorphic knowledge frames. Translators must be aware, however, that cognitive frames don't have to be isomorphic. Lexical items don't always point to congruent regions within the larger frame. For instance, even between the relatively isomorphic German and American commercial event frames, there are differences. An American might say *I bought a new car* or *I bought a new house*. The speaker does not imply that he paid the full price for house or car. In America the region accessed by the associational structure of *to buy* and *car* and *house* may extend to further linkages with concepts such as *mortgage* or *installment loan*. These further linkages are not as well established in German culture, and the use of the word *kaufen* may not access these peripheral knowledge regions at all. The copresence of the words *buy* and *house* in an English text create an association, a composite meaning, which is not identical with the composite meaning created by the copresence in the German text of their linguistic equivalents. These differences are negligible compared to the striking differences encountered if one attempts to map the commercial event frames of the Middle East against German or American frames (Hall 1959, 117–119). There the verb *to cost* and the noun *price* do not necessarily imply fixed amounts which the seller will charge and which the buyer will have to pay. The knowledge structure pointed to by these lexical items involves notions of bargaining and negotiation which are not parts of the German or American frame structure.

Matching cultural frames is an extremely important and difficult translation task. The translator's objective is to use the text, and the associative structures created within it by networks of lexical items, to map frames. Words in English such as *cost, spend, charge, profit, bargain, overcharge,* and *underbid* may not have exact equivalents in Arabic because the commercial event frame is organized differently and has different contents. The translator must analyze the structure and contents of the source and target frames and create a mapping which brings associations of English words into their closest approximation with associations of Arabic words. It may be necessary to use textual expansions to clarify the fact that the knowledge structures referenced by so-called equivalents are not, in fact, congruent.

Fillmore has also spoken of interactional frames: "a categorization of the distinguishable contents of interaction in which speakers of a language can expect to find themselves, together with information about the appropriate linguistic choices relevant to these interactions" (Fillmore 1976, 25).

He cites, as a typical case, what he calls the *greeting frame*, which shows wide variation from culture to culture. The specific textual form of a greeting and its complementary response are selected from a restricted inventory of topics and expressions and are often determined by highly specific contextual conditions. There is no clear distinction between cognitive and interactional frames. It is true that many greetings are purely interactional; *how do you do, hi, hello, good morning,* and *yo!* are, in fact, no more than signals functioning as a kind of social mortar for phatic communion. As soon as we probe deeper into the social matrix of greetings, with their names, titles, and other forms of address, we must account for a variety of conceptual distinctions involving social role and social stratification. What surfaces here is the subtle shading of frame semantics into frame pragmatics. We must consider, for instance, how the passage of time determines the accessing of greeting frames such as *good morning, good afternoon, good evening,* and *good night.*

Cognitive frames don't just reflect socially distributed cognitive patterns related to characteristic distributions of linguistic material. They may also contain overt implications for the interactional scenarios in which the linguistic items are used. Still, it is useful to distinguish between cognitive and interactional frames. It is then possible to use the interaction frame concept to explain the categorization and social distribution of textual forms. A greeting is no less a text than an instruction manual, legal contract, or industrial patent. All are structured forms of interaction with *distinguishable contents* that are used under specific contextual conditions. Thus, the frame concept includes both cognitive-conceptual and communicative-interactional features. Interactional frames provide recipes for producing and decoding texts. These texts are frameworks into which linguistic indices to cognitive frames are injected (by writer or translator) and from which linguistic indices to cognitive frames may be extracted (by reader and translation user). The distinction is structurally useful, but it may not be psychologically real. Regardless of their contents, frames may be regarded as integrated socially distributed patterns of conceptualizing and interacting in social reality using language.

The lexical items in texts usually index many different frames; the text creates an associational structure that is a composite structure comprised of all the frame regions referenced by the text. The text serves as an organizational mechanism, establishing actual links between frame contents whose prior association was only potential. Virtual associations are converted to actual associations using textual mechanisms. Indirect linguistic copresence is the mechanism for pairing virtual elements within and between frames.

The names for meals in English are certainly elements of some frame or frames. If breakfast is understood as the first meal in a day, and lunch as a meal to be eaten at midday, then the words function within a temporal frame as a means for referring to divisions of the day. Breakfast is identified as an element in a temporally structured pattern of meals. The dominant relationship within the frame is *time ordering*, and the word *breakfast* functions within the frame as a means of ordering the day. In the sentence, *We had a cooked breakfast,* the time element is essential for comprehension, since it is necessary to reference the concept of *first meal of the day.* A paraphrase could be, *We had something cooked as first meal (of the day).*

The same word could be associated with the particular combination of foods people of a community are familiar with and tend to eat for breakfast. Note the difference between an English breakfast, an American breakfast, and a continental breakfast. Here the dominant relationship in the associational structure is not temporal. Rather, it is a culture-bound association of elements, a traditional pattern. What this indicates is that the lexical item *breakfast* may refer to more than one frame. For instance, if a cafe sign carries the advertisement *breakfast served at any time,* then the temporal frame is blocked or minimized. The textual situation selects an alternate frame where we are to understand breakfast as a particular combination of foods.[19]

In the first case, the word breakfast operates *functionally* as a temporal marker, and in the second it acts as a specific mechanism for *associating* other elements. There are other possibilities. If a child begins to use the word *ball,* she may link it with a frame element (concept) standing for a *particular set of things played with in particular settings and with particular people* (Fillmore 1976, 21). It is functionally related to other objects. As children get older, they learn to restrict the word *ball* to *spherical* and *bounceable* things. This kind of frame is based on *criterial* relationships. Terminology systems typically reference criterial frames. Witness the shift from the child's use of *aunt (Tante)* and *uncle (Onkel)* as a reference for any grown-up friend or neighbor (functioning in opposition to parent) to the clear-cut references that emerge from an adult's understanding of the criterially-based kinship system. Understanding the criterial bases for scientific and technical terminologies is a crucial element in the successful translation of scientific and technical texts. Most technical terminologies are highly structured artificial cognitive frames.

Individual words can never be understood and cannot be translated outside of their frame references. Frame references are always embedded in texts. The meaning potential of a word is determined by its role as an active ingredient in a text. Of course, because the frame systems of L_1 producers and L_2 comprehenders are different, the translator has to somehow compensate. What has been traditionally referred to as linguistic non-correspondence, the case where linguistic items in the L_1 and their so-called foreign "equivalents" don't match, is actually caused by the fact their frames are not congruent. Non-correspondence is not just a linguistic phenomenon; it is also a cognitive and textual one. The translator must try to overcome the problems that arise from trying to reconcile different framing systems by making sure that the target text activates, if possible, those elements in the L_2 frame that most closely match the elements of the L_1 frame activated by the source text.

Note what happens in translations of two sample texts (Fillmore 1976, 27). Two men who had spent a very short period of time in San Francisco write home to their individual families: *I spent two hours on land this afternoon* and *I spent two hours on the ground this afternoon*. The first example requires the reader to retrieve the frame for sea voyages. It contains, among other items, one of the two distinct states expressed by the phrases *on land* and *at sea*. The equivalent German sea voyages frame would be referenced by the phrases *an Land* and *auf See*. The other case activates the air travel frame with the two mutually exclusive states of being *on the ground* and *in the air*. In German, however, potential "equivalents" such as *auf dem Boden, am Boden, auf der Erde,* and *auf dem Erdboden* do not always work as opposites to *in der Luft* because they do not reference, automatically, the air travel frame. The translator will have to use the word *unten* or some other lexical reference to evoke the same frame in the same way. For instance, a non-specialist will more often distinguish *unten* and *oben* in this context. Sometimes one may find *Das Flugzeug war schon nicht mehr auf der Erde als*. . . . Not uncommon is *nicht in der Luft* for *on the ground*. The German air travel frame has an internal structure which does not so clearly oppose the two states.[20] Thus, more appropriate translations for the first sample text might be *Ich war heute nachmittag zwei Stunden unten* or *Ich war heute nachmittag zwei Stunden nicht in der Luft.*[21]

The translation variants underscore another difference. The English originals with their first person agent, their past tense (*spent*), and their time-deictic expression (*this afternoon*) put the writers' experience into a temporal relationship with the time of writing. The comprehender can unambiguously deduce that the letters were written at sea or in the air.

Translations have to incorporate this kind of implicit information. There is often no explicit expression of such relationships in the text. They must be inferred by the reader, who uses his or her knowledge of lexical and grammatical structures. The German simple past *war* could just as well be replaced by the so-called conversational past, *bin gewesen,* both implying unambiguously, just as the English original does, a state in the past that is discontinuous in relation to the present experience of writing. Thus, the translation provides exactly the same information as the original even though it might be necessary to alter the grammatical expression at the textual surface.

These simple examples point out that the textual process of translation requires an ability to match the L_1 sender's and the L_2 receiver's mechanisms for framing experience. Linguistic knowledge of both the L_1 and the L_2 is necessary but not sufficient. The translator must be aware of framing differences and understand how linguistic and textual processes attach to frame-based knowledge. Translations, ideally, should be the kind of texts that L_1 senders would have formulated for L_2 audiences themselves.

Scenarios, Schemas, Plans, Scripts

Frames provide the translation theorist with a mechanism for talking about how language can reference regions of cultural experience. The concept is powerful because linguistic elements in a text can provide access to all sorts of implicit knowledge carried in the frame. This can occur even though only a fragment of the frame, referenced by a specific linguistic index, was named in the text. A frame is *activated* by a textual reference. Activation makes available the contents of the frame and opens access to other frames.

The concept of frame we have used so far is a static one. Frames are an abstraction, a way of conceiving of the internal organization of human cognition. There is a dynamic aspect to frames. Frames may be organized into sequences, patterns, or networks. The progress of a reader through a text is paralleled by a simultaneous navigation of a frame-structured knowledge network. The text establishes associative links between frames and between the elements of frames. The navigation of the nodes and links of computer hypertext is an apt analogy. The dynamic aspect of frames has been expressed in the concepts of *schema, plan, script, and scenario*. Scenarios may be understood as *programmed frame structures*, organizational structures which establish progressions and connections between frames at the time of frame actualization.

In the sentence, *he gave a generous tip*, the word *tip* activates the experience of one person giving money to another person in the restaurant frame. A person who hears the text with the word *tip* in it can infer that someone has ordered something to eat, has eaten it, has paid for it, and has given additional money to the waiter or waitress. The amount of the tip may even be inferred. It is, as a rule, lower than the actual price of the meal, and in certain countries it may be calculated as a percentage of the cost of the meal. The method of presentation may vary by country. In America the tip is left on the table, but in Germany the custom is to give the waiter a composite sum (price plus tip) and then say *es stimmt* or *stimmt so*. This means that no change is expected.[22]

The "restaurant" frame accessed by the word *tip* includes knowledge of conventional sequences of events, actions, states, and processes that can be used with sequences of words and constructions to impose order upon texts. The frame item *tip* is linked to a global structure that enables communicators to process connected discourse. This global structure or *scenario* has been abstracted from experience. It has been simultaneously internalized and named by senders and receivers as an activity conditioned by community co-membership. The concept is related to the idea of a *typical course-of-action* formulated by Schutz (1970). When texts are produced and understood, frames and their organizing scenarios are used. Texts are complex structures where cognitive elements, organized by scenarios, are represented by linguistic structures.

The scenario concept is relevant to translation. For instance, consider the term *alimony* from the civil law frame. It is usually defined as regular payments that a man has been legally ordered to pay to his former wife after they have been separated or divorced. The German term *Unterhalt(sbeitrag)* should adequately reference this legal obligation in any textual scenario. But what about the translation of the following news item from the *American Daily News* of February 19, 1976 (Barnhart et al. 1980, 342)?

> The Lee Marvin palimony case ... shows that—married or not—people who live together cannot avoid a shared responsibility.

Palimony is a neologism originally coined as a slang expression during the seventies in the United States. It was borrowed by journalists in Great Britain and is now quite frequently used in British newspapers. The problem for the translator is that while *Unterhaltungszahlung* establishes the civil law frame in German, the German scenario is different. The pre-existing connections between frame elements invoked by the alimony scenario are different connections in German. Because of differences in the legal system, it is not implicit in the reference that money could be paid to some unmarried persons one might have lived with. A possible translation of the text is:

> Aus dem Prozeß über die Unterhaltszahlung, in den (der amerikanische Filmschauspieler) Lee Marvin verwickelt ist ... geht hervor, daß Verheiratete oder Unverheiratete gleichermaßen, wenn sie zusammenleben, sich ihrer gegenseitigen Verantwortung nicht entziehen können.

The translation generalizes *alimony* and *palimony*, which correctly represents the legal state of affairs. Two role relations in the scenario, ex-husband and ex-wife, and man and mistress, are reduced to one. The particular text evidently supports this neutralization. But what if the linguistic context (*married or not*) is missing? Then the translator will have to supply it as a *paraphrase* or other *frame extension*.

There is a methodological distinction between frame and scenario which may have become a bit blurred in our discussion. Frames are learned, at least in part, from texts. Frames are activated as part of text production, but they may have a mental existence outside of texts. Scenarios put frames into action in texts. Scenarios are not just larger or more complex frames; they are the mechanisms for *activating* the contents of frames. They may be interpreted as *abstract texts* when they serve as an underlying semantic structure for a textual sequence. Abstract texts do not represent any particular text but refer to recurrent phenomenal patterns. They are an event or situation prototype which can be textually expressed.

Scenarios can be further subdivided into *schemas*. Although definitions vary, a schema refers to that part of a scenario which can be isolated as a more or less discrete pattern of objects, events, states, and processes linked by time, place, or causal relations. Several schemas may compose a scenario. A text processing issue which has not yet been resolved is the relationship between the progression of schemas and the semantic and syntactic surface structuring of texts. Social interactions using language show recurrent patterns at the beginning, middle, and end of encounters. These discrete patterns, for instance, in a conversation, in a lecture, or in a sermon, are supported by specific schemas. They are, like scenarios, internalized knowledge structures enabling language users to produce and comprehend texts. Some theorists have spoken of *plans* and *scripts*.[23] These terms represent a further classification of the knowledge structures underlying the processing of texts. Nevertheless, in the interest of greater clarity, we will not discuss these in great detail. Plans are basically goal-oriented scenarios; scripts are essentially highly conventional scenarios.

Translators have to account for the knowledge organization that scenarios and schemas provide. If they do not, there is a risk that the reader's progression through the text will go astray. The linguistic patterns of the target do not just cue associations of knowledge elements in frames. They cue progressions through them. The translator must control this progression explicitly.

The translation theorist also has to account for scenarios in the form of plans. The idea of a goal-oriented progression through a knowledge network coincides with the way in which the translator activates the translation process. The translator's courses-of-action in approaching the translation, which have been learned by experience and training, are a goal-oriented traversal of frames. The frames contain knowledge of language, knowledge of texts, knowledge of first-level translation procedures, and world knowledge. In the act of translation, the translator activates translation competence using a translation plan. One important task of an empirical translation studies would be to observe practicing translators and examine the differences and similarities in the translation plans they put into practice.

THREE

Textuality

Textuality and "Textness"

The translator is a mediator in the process of bilingual communication. Translation creates the possibility for people to understand one another across languages and across cultures. The process of translation is a textual process that connects one knowledge system with another. The translator makes the connection by inserting linguistic indices in the target text. These indices give the L_2 reader access to the underlying knowledge structure of the author's original message. Translators must link L_1 frames and scenarios with corresponding L_2 frames and scenarios using the L_2 linguistic system. Results of this matching process have to be L_2 texts. The translation has to compete in the target text world as a natural example of an L_2 text, and it must exhibit all of the features which make it recognizable as a native text.

Mediation is a demanding task. Translators need an orienting principle to guide them in the translation process. The principle should emphasize the importance of texts as representations of abstract knowledge structures. It should remind the translator that the final translation is not a static object but a dynamic mechanism for transmitting and activating knowledge. The organizing principle must account for the transfer of knowledge into texts and the retrieval of knowledge from texts. It should be "linguistic" enough to allow empirical approaches to the underlying cognitive system, but it should not be restricted to a registration of the formal devices of the two languages.

From its inception, modern text linguistics has been searching for an orienting principle. The principle of *textuality* is the most promising candidate to date. Textuality integrates translation procedure and world knowledge with the text as product. Textuality refers to the complex set of features that texts must have to be considered texts. Textuality is a property that a complex linguistic object assumes when it reflects certain social and communicative constraints. The operation of these constraints is manifested in recognizable linguistic patterns at the textual surface. Textuality can also be seen as the state of "textness" that a translator tries to induce in the target text. If translation is a complex problem-solving activity, then textuality is the goal-state toward which the process is working. In the context of translation studies, the principle of textuality can be used to define the conditions under which an L_1 text and its L_2 counterpart can be said to be textually equivalent.

What are these conditions? It is not enough to say that textuality is a complex property that separates texts from non-texts. What specific features combine to create textuality? The effective translator must understand the elements that combine to create textuality if he or she is to manipulate them in the interests of the target text reader. A linguistic analysis of the text can never fully reveal its textuality. The linguistic surface of a text activates chains of references to knowledge frames; this complex activation induces a recognition of "textness" in the reader. Textuality is induced by the linguistic surface but is not confined to it. The linguistic surface of a text is no more than a pointer to its textuality.[24] In this chapter, we will examine seven broad characteristics of texts which combine to produce the complex property of textuality. The seven features are: intentionality, acceptability, situationality, informativity, coherence, cohesion, and intertextuality.

Intentionality

The following is an excerpt from the British *Highway Code*. We present it as an example of a text which possesses intentionality, the first of the seven features of textuality. Published by Her Majesty's Stationary Office, the Code is an official list of rules recommended for British drivers. It is not a body of law as, for instance, the *Straßenverkehrsordnung* of the former German Democratic Republic. The document is a small booklet with three parts: the *Highway Code* proper, an appendix entitled *Signs and Signals*, and *The Law Demands*, a section dealing with major points of the various Acts and Regulations which have been sanctioned by British law.[25] The opening section and the first two rules of part 2 of the code are cited:

THE ROAD USER ON WHEELS

TO ALL DRIVERS AND RIDERS and in general to those in charge of horses

16. Before you move off, make sure that you can do so safely and without inconvenience to other road users. Watch particularly the road behind. Make the proper signal before moving out, and give way to passing and overtaking vehicles.

17. KEEP WELL TO THE LEFT, except when you intend to overtake or turn right. Do not hug the middle of the road.

Drivers in Britain can clearly make sense of this text. Its authors at the Ministry of Transport know their subject and audience. The authors also have a goal for their communicative behavior: they are trying to make the roads safer. Their linguistic behavior is not random; it is directed. This global *interactional aim* is reflected in the structure of the text. The multiple sections, their headings, the use of capitalization, and the division of sections into rules reflect purpose and planning. The multiple sections are textual realizations of sub-goals in a plan to influence driver behavior. The profile of the text reflects a set of *intentions*. If the text had not been intended to achieve some result, it would never have been written or published. The *intent to do something* belongs to the communicative event. It is a fundamental element of the textuality of the sequence of discourse called the *Highway Code*.

A characteristic feature of textuality is called *intentionality*. Admittedly, this section from the Highway Code is an exceptional example of intentionality because the structure of the textual surface clearly reflects its underlying purposes. Is intentionality really such a fundamental textual property that its absence would destroy the textuality of a text? Can we really say that in order for communication to occur, the intentions of the sender must always be fully understood? Such a statement would not be realistic. We must distinguish an author's *productive intentions* from the indications of intentionality realized in the patterned sequence of linguistic signs at the textual surface. The writer's intentions are ephemeral, but they leave a mark or trace on the text. When the writer's intentions were active, they helped to shape the text. They were critical factors at the early stages of the text production process when overall plan and ideational sequence were formulated. At the time of writing, the sender wanted to do something, to achieve certain results which had been projected. This desire to have "effect," to achieve something with the text, shapes the profile of the text. Linguistic sequences which assert, question, enjoin, insult, persuade, report, convince, or instruct are constructed in order to do something. Some scholars express an extreme view that a translator can only translate what can be inferred from the surface of the text. Others, equally extreme, claim that one has to translate what the author "really" meant. This disagreement should not deter us from looking for the truth somewhere in the middle ground. Intentionality is meant to sensitize us to the correlation between intentions and texts.

There are many highly conventional texts where format and sense clearly indicate the underlying purpose. Texts like formulaic greetings, socially sanctioned signs and announcements, and ritualized messages are examples. Instruction manuals, patents, and legal contracts likewise clearly indicate their underlying intentionality. At the other end of the spectrum are difficult poetic texts whose intentions are more obscure.

The notion of textually realized intentionality cannot include the entire complex set of particular intentions underlying the communicative interaction. Indeed, sometimes the intentionality perceived in a text is not necessarily the same as the author's intentionality. A *faux pas* is a text where productive intent and receptive intent have diverged. Text comprehenders can only retrieve from the text what they recognize as having been put in. In addition, the reader's purposeful orientation to the text is a reflection of receptive intent. From the reader's point of view, intentionality is connected with *relevance,* a measure of the importance he or she attaches to the information. A text in a technical journal intended for experts has a very specific intentionality. Readers of the L_1 text and L_2 translation judge it from their own interactional perspective. They attend to (and care about) only those elements which relate to their communicative purposes in the exchange. In pragmatic texts, author intent and receiver intent are usually a close match. These two types of intent diverge only when the execution of the text is faulty. In these cases the text (or portions of it) does not do what it is supposed to do. Intentionality and relevance are a sender-receiver (translator-receiver) pairing. Before a translation is begun, a translator must be aware of what makes the text relevant to the audience. The translator needs to know how this relevance relates to the intentionality displayed in the L_1 text. Intentionality is not really about an author's intent, because sometimes the text does not accomplish what the author intends. Intentionality is about the effects of an author's or translator's decisions on the text and their subsequent impact on the receptive intentions of the reader.

Acceptability

Intentionality is associated with acceptability. The author's original goals in writing the text cannot be achieved if the reader cannot figure out what the text is supposed to do. For a text to be received as a piece of purposeful linguistic communication, it must be seen and accepted as a text. Acceptability does not necessarily imply that the receiver believe the specific contents of the text. It does require that the addressee be able to identify and extract those contents. Even though listeners and readers have become accustomed to a wide variation in the form of texts, there are limits. The receiver must be able to determine what kind of text the sender intended to send, and what was to be achieved by sending it.

There is no single norm for acceptability. All texts are subject to constraints; otherwise they would not be recognizable as texts. There is wide variation. Some categories of texts are quite constrained, and others are not. To be acceptable, an official text such as the *Highway Code* must possess particular textual features, including standard grammatical and lexical patterning. The writer of the *Highway Code* has less freedom than the participants in an informal roadside conversation (even if they are discussing the same topics discussed in the Code). Consider the following passage from the Road Traffic Act, 1972, Section 37:

> A failure on the part of any person to observe a provision of the highway code shall not of itself render that person liable to criminal proceedings of any kind, but any such failure may in any proceedings (whether civil or criminal, and including proceedings for an offense under this Act, the Road Traffic regulation Act 1967 or the Public Passenger Vehicles Act 1981) be relied upon by any party to the proceedings as tending to establish or to negate any liability which is in question in those proceedings.

If a translator is to produce an acceptable target text from this source text, he or she must first understand the acceptability standards of the L_2 community for this particular category of text. This is not difficult if L_1 and L_2 language users have the same acceptability standards for the text type. In most cases standards of textual acceptability differ. The German *Straßenverkehrsordnung*, which functions as an equivalent to the *Road Traffic Act* because it has a corresponding intentionality, is governed by different acceptability conditions. The translator cannot render the target text's typical grammatical and lexical usages into the source language uncritically. For instance, should the translator delete the English text's second person references and introduce the German *Farhzeugführer* in their place? Further, the metaphorical *hug the middle of the road*, acceptable in the English text, is out of place in an official German text. Should it be deleted or rephrased? Consider the distinction between drivers and riders. This distinction is not made in the corresponding paragraphs of the *Straßenverkehrsordnung*.[26] The inclusion of *those in charge of horses*, which evidently reflected a substantial horse population in 1954 England, contrasts with *Gespannführer* and the generalized *Personen* who are charged with *Führen und Treiben von Tieren* in the *Straßenverkehrsordnung*. German road users accept and expect a different set of textual conventions in their official texts. A German reader's expectations have been shaped by a unique textual experience. German textual expectations are a product of the historical development of texts in the society. Textual acceptability functions as an organizing and stabilizing element in social relations. This stability lets acceptability standards be used in the presumptions of mutual knowledge that are preconditions for the exchange of texts.

Anthropologists and sociolinguists have studied textual conventions as part of ethnic studies. They have isolated and described linguistic rituals with strict acceptability standards. However, all texts exhibit acceptability standards. These standards are a part of textuality in both industrial and traditional societies. Generations of translators have had to cope with the need to make their translation product, the L_2 text, acceptable to an audience that does not know the conventions which govern the L_1 text. Acceptability is a primary characteristic of texts. In some approaches to translation it is the primary consideration. *Recipient-oriented translation* always modifies the nature of the text in the interest of the target reader (Holz-Mänttäri 1984; Vermeer 1986).

Principle of Cooperation

Acceptability and intentionality are components of textuality, and they are orienting principles for translation. They cannot act alone to establish textuality. For texts to be accepted as they were intended (or, at least, as intentional), they must be negotiated. This negotiation implies an agreement to cooperate in communication. For instance, in direct conversation participants make a conscious effort to cooperate in making themselves understood. Similarly, the professional interpreter mediating between L_1 and L_2 speakers must rely on their cooperation. Grice first formulated what he called the *co-operative principle* to describe negotiation in conversation (Grice 1975, 45–46). Yet, since linguistic communication is always interactional, this principle could be extended to cover all kinds of spoken and written discourse, even if co-operation is indirect. Speakers and writers operate under the impression that there exists (or will exist) an actual or potential addressee who will accept uttered words or written lines as inducements to enter into communication. Texts are invitations to communicate and must be presented to listeners and readers in ways which secure their cooperation and comprehension. Acceptability is a precondition for cooperation, and the presumption of cooperation is a rationale for adhering to acceptability standards.

Many texts are displaced in time and space; they do not have the immediacy of face-to-face communication. Clearly, there is no actual cooperation between the writer of a computer instruction manual and its reader. Reading such a text does involve a cooperative mental attitude. There is a disposition to cooperate, regardless of displacement in time and location, that orients and leads the reader to accept the text. The text, for its part, must display features which induce the reader to enter into, and remain a part of, the communication. The principle of cooperation explains the willingness of the L_2 text user to negotiate the meaning of the text and to accept it as a text. The negotiation can occur even if the original sender of the text is unknown and may never have projected the L_2 reader as an audience. Cooperation is a precondition of translatability and a presumption the translator must make. Lack of cooperation can be a source of failure. Improper translation is a failure to convince the reader to participate in the textual interaction. It is a violation of the principle of cooperation. Cooperation is more than just a philosophical issue. Violating the principle has practical consequences for the translator.

Maxim of Quantity

Grice derived several instructive maxims from the principle of cooperation (Grice 1975; Neubert 1983, 109). The first of these is the maxim of quantity (Grice 1975, 45):

> Make your contribution as informative as is required. Do not make your contribution more informative than is required.

Usually L_1 text producers have L_1 readers in mind when they create their texts. Translators are also subject to the maxim of quantity when they recreate their texts for L_2 readers. For instance, there are cases where a translator has to expand or compress the wording of the L_2 text relative to corresponding structures in the L_1 text. This is stipulated by differences in the linguistic systems and differences in frame organization. It may be that a meaning implied in the L_1 is not implied in a potential L_2 rendering. The maxim of quantity advises the translator to assess the information requirements of the L_2 as a text in its own right and make adjustments to compensate. The maxim of quantity may be applied to grammatical structures in translation. Schmidt has given extensive treatment to the problem of condensing complicated Russian grammatical constructions into (usually) simpler German constructions (Schmidt 1982). In Russian to German translation, there is always the possibility of using one-to-one, structure-for-structure renderings. Often these translations appear verbose to the L_2 reader. In extreme cases they impede understanding. The translator may have to resort to using translation procedures like *compression* or *omission*. The translator makes this decision as a textual negotiation in the interests of the L_2 reader; the reader expects certain grammatical structures and not others. Compression assists the flow of information. It secures the reader's cooperation and provides a basis for accepting the text. Some of the information contained in the Russian grammatical constructions may not be necessary in the given translation situation. The user may not need the information. The maxim of quantity advises the translator to use translation procedures that produce target texts that best serve their readers.

The maxim of quantity also applies to lexical choice in translation. There are cases where the L_1 text incorporates a condensed representation of some sociocultural experience typical of the L_1 community. Typical examples are the names of institutions (*Grand Old Party*), people (*Old Blue Eyes*), and historical events (*Watergate*). The translator may choose to use a paraphrase or explicitation instead of bringing the item over as a direct loan. This method is advisable where *realia* appear in the source text. A good translator will almost invariably supply extra information in the L_2 text. The L_2 community does not share the mutual knowledge necessary to make the appropriate references to social, cultural, and geographical phenomena.[27]

There is an important implication in the maxim of quantity. Each linguistic system provides a certain pool of grammatical and lexical resources for coding information. The use of these resources is textually specific within a language. As a result, translations can be larger or smaller than their corresponding source texts. Translations from English into German are almost always longer than the English originals. The maxim of quantity frees translators from the delusion that they must maintain textual parity. Although the translator is liberated in this regard, the maxim of quantity also requires the translator to avoid adding unnecessary words and phrases. This is especially true if the translator is not acquainted with appropriate L_2 equivalents. The maxim of quantity is not a license to digress and paraphrase when there are unambiguous and functional renderings that also serve the purposes of the translation. This kind of misplaced expansion is common in translations of technical and scientific material by novices. If there is a one-to-one correspondence between L_1 and L_2 technical terms (e.g., *Tellerfeder* and *diaphragm spring* in automotive technology), then the direct equivalent should be used. The novice translator's habit of padding, done to make the translation more readable for a general public, is actually misleading.[28] If the translator's audience is a group of automotive experts, general explanations are not going to be particularly useful. Of course, one must assume that the translator has not been asked to popularize the material. In this case, the situation may clearly call for the addition of information. The purpose of the text plays a significant role in determining its functionality. Some translation theorists have claimed that "purpose is the dominant factor in all translation" (Reiß and Vermeer 1984). The use of the maxim of quantity, and all of the maxims and advisories presented in this text, proceed from the fundamental principle that the translation situation determines the translation procedures that should be applied. Choice of L_2 lexical items is not just a question of availability in the L_2 vocabulary. It is also a question of text-specific frame selection. If lexical choices in the L_2 invoke frames that are similar in content to L_1 frames, then expansions and compressions will be rare. If there is a low level of correspondence, expansions or compressions cannot be avoided. The maxim of quantity must always be followed in response to the requirements of a particular text in its translation situation.

Maxim of Quality

Grice formulated a second maxim which supports acceptability and the principle of cooperation (Grice 1975, 46). It is the maxim of quality: *Try to make your contribution one that is true*. This is a difficult request. Direct application of the maxim takes it for granted that texts transmit nothing but factual information. It assumes that we can determine what the truth is. The maxim certainly holds true for scientific communication. The maxim instructs the translator to maintain the (sometimes disputed) rule that a translator must correct mistakes in the original text instead of perpetuating them in the L_2 (Newmark 1983). But is the translator always in a position to judge? Can the translator recognize the mistakes? Are all facts known? Is a textual deviation from the truth intentional? There is a fine distinction between facts and opinions and between opinions and outright lies. When we consider other kinds of texts, like editorials and newspaper articles, the application of this "the truth and nothing but the truth" approach becomes problematic. This does not imply that such texts contain falsehoods. In texts, truth takes on a special meaning.

> Making statements descriptive of states-of-affairs is but one of the functions of language; that it also serves, as do our other customs and patterns of behavior, the establishment and maintenance of social relationships and for the expression of our attitudes and personality. (Lyons 1977, 50)

Texts carry meaning and have an underlying propositional structure. This propositional framework is the ideational structure referred to in the previous chapter; it is a linked set of references that organizes the text's information content into a coherent pattern. Cresswell has spoken of propositions as a function from a possible world to a truth value (Cresswell 1973, 94). Cresswell expands on the notion: "if we think for a moment of the job a proposition has to do, we see that it must be something which can be true or false, not only in the actual world, but in each possible world" (Cresswell 1973, 23).

We have already introduced the notion of possible world in our discussion of linguistic copresence. Let us assume that texts make representations about possible worlds, and that these worlds can act as substitutes for reality. This means that the truth of assertions made in texts may be judged against the objects, states, events, or processes attributed to that world. Thus, the opinions and beliefs, even the lies, in a political speech may be true in the context of the possible world that is represented. Jaako Hintikka has simply referred to a possible world as a "possible state of affairs" (Hintikka 1962). Texts are produced to represent states of affairs. The maxim of quality requires the translator to preserve the internal truth-consistency of the text. References to objects, events, places, and people must have an internal consistency. The truth of the source text, discounting obvious factual errors and typographical mistakes, is taken by the translator as a given. The translator is obligated to do nothing unless he or she discovers internal inconsistency. These are violations of the virtual world created in the text. Such a stance is essentially value-free. There are translators who argue, with some justification, that it is necessary to evaluate the source text and weigh its moral and ideological values. They want to determine whether the text is "worthy of translation." Such arguments aside, for most pragmatic texts translation is a *truth-preserving transformation*.[29] In cases where the purposes of the target text diverge appreciably from those of the source, the maxim of quality urges us to create internal consistency in the target. In these cases, translation is a *truth-creating transformation*.

Maxim of Relation

Grice's third maxim deals with the semantic and linguistic relations that exist between textual elements. Some of the elements and relations are more important than others. They relate more directly to the main ideas of the text; they reflect the essential content the author intended to communicate. In this third maxim Grice admonishes us *to be relevant*. The maxim advises us to render the target text in such a way that the reader may disregard irrelevant detail and recognize those elements which belong to the primary ideational structure. Most substantial texts contain a large number of sense relationships. Comprehension will be enhanced if the textual profile is manipulated in such a way that the reader is able to focus on some relations and discount others.

The quest for relevance does not imply that only certain parts of a text are crucial, and other less important parts may be discarded. To be relevant means that the sender, and by extension the translator, has to make evident what the primary contents of the text are. Many assertions and statements made when developing a topic are of minor importance relative to topicalizing statements put forward at critical points in the discourse. Secondary or tertiary elements may provide additional contextual, attitudinal, expressive, or social information in support of the main point. They may serve to introduce, to specify, or to generalize a main idea. All of these supporting elements are relevant textually. It is just that they are at a different level of relevance. If a sentence or sentence group that presents secondary ideas is deleted, the text may still be understandable. If a deletion involves a primary idea, the text may lose its internal consistency. The translator can use linguistic and textual resources to indicate the relative importance of text segments. The idea that there are levels of relevance implies that there may be irrelevant (or nearly irrelevant) parts of a text. How does one determine when an item is not relevant? One criterion might be that an element is irrelevant when it does not contribute to the development of the text. Another criterion might specify that an element is irrelevant if it does not further the overall interactional aim. A proper determination of relevance implies an assessment of the intentionality of the text. It is the translator's responsibility to create in the L_2 text a network of sense relations that corresponds to the relevance structure of the L_1 text. The reader of a translation should be led to make the same decisions or come to the same conclusions as a reader of the L_1 text. If the purpose of the translation has changed, the translator must create a new relevance structure reflecting the receptive intentionality (needs) of the target audience. The same main ideas should appear, appropriately modified, introduced, or developed by supporting textual elements.

A simple example involves newspaper articles and their headlines. The headline usually provides textually significant information; it functions as a pointer to the main ideas of the body of the text. If the headline does not reflect the main ideas of the text, the reader may be misled. Sometimes, instead of building a headline by abstracting the content of the piece, an editor will use or coin phrases that are meant to catch the reader's attention. The translator should have no problem with headlines that directly reflect the main ideas of the text. Headlines such as *Rail unions plan war on cuts* or *Profits leap while economy slumps*, or even *Dog's lucky day*, clearly indicate what the reader can expect (*Morning Star*, 21 September 1983). The headline *New row over QE2* lends itself nicely to an expanded German translation: *Erneut Streit um Neuausstattung der Queen Elisabeth II*. These headlines follow the maxim of relation and are semantically linked to the main bodies of their respective texts.

However, headlines such as *United States: Showing the Flag* (*Time*, 22 August 1983) and *Sense at all costs* (*The Times Literary Supplement*, 12 August 1983) are only obliquely related to the relevant themes of the articles they label. Their meaning is utterly dependent upon what is contained in the succeeding passages. The meaning of the headline emerges only after the reader has read the article. In the first example, *showing the flag* is idiomatic and metaphoric. It conveys the idea of *being present at an event or at a place in order to show solidarity with others*. A political connotation may be added to this: *making clear what one's opinions are, especially to support them against opposition*. An L_1 reader of this headline, equipped with a knowledge of his or her language and of American political affairs, can predict the major themes of the news article. The subtitle *Not since Vietnam has the U.S. flexed so much muscle abroad,* also metaphorical, indicates additional main ideas by adding a military dimension. By the maxim of relation, the sentences of the first paragraph should elaborate inferences that the L_1 reader has made from reading the headline:

> For a country at peace, the U.S. is throwing its military weight around a lot these days. To be sure, no American soldiers are on the attack anywhere in the world. But the U.S. has a remarkable portion of its troops, ships, and planes around the planet, including contingents from every branch of the service deployed on three continents, well within shooting distance of hot combat zones—Lebanon, Chad, Central America.

The relevance structure of the headline *Showing the Flag* is supported by the text. The orienting function of the headline should remain the same in a translation. But a rendering of the idiom by its German counterpart, *die Flagge zeigen,* has a distinct and unintended nautical connotation. This intrusive meaning is a semantic problem. The English headline also poses grammatical problems for the translator. German headline grammar (a textual convention related to acceptability) requires that a noun express the subject of the action. *USA zeigen die Flagge* is one possibility. Alternatively, the phrase could be nominalized, as in *Das Zeigen der Flagge.* This last alternative would not be intelligible or relevant to the reader. The semantic discrepancy is more serious than the grammatical problem. The L_2 reader needs to be able to recover the senses of *being present* and *making a demonstrative show* which are parts of the main ideational structure. The translator also needs to express the military connotations of the subtitle *flexed so much muscle.* Military connotations permeate the article. The translator must attempt to inject this relevant information into the headline. He or she must ensure that the headline-story relationship that exists in the L_1 text is preserved in the L_2 text (even under L_2 acceptability standards). One solution might be *Weltweite militärische Präsenz der USA.* The adjective *weltweit* makes the headline more explicit and underscores its relevance to what follows. Adherence to the maxim of relation leads the translator to a reconstruction of the sense relationships of the L_1 text by exploiting the L_2 user's linguistic and world knowledge.

Solutions are not always simple. The headline *Sense at all costs* is an idiolectic phrase typical of its source, *The Times Literary Supplement*. It expresses the reviewer's opinion of a book, the title of which appears below the headline (Donald Spence, *Narrative Truth and Historical Truth*). Like most headlines in this weekly journal, the style is terse, simple, and incisive.[30] A mundane expression or phrase such as *at all costs* is given an unexpected meaning by its atypical association with another lexical item, *sense*. The association is unusual because the two items do not usually occur together. This unusual collocation is eventually accounted for in the text of the review. The reviewer criticizes the author's attempt to dismantle psychoanalytic theory while using its methods. The word *sense*, used at the beginning of the review to indicate the futility of the search for meaning (historical truth), is then associated with the author's insistence that the truth of psychoanalysis patient narratives (narrative truth) should not be dismissed.

If the discerning reader has followed the reviewer's argument, he or she may be able to interpret the headline. The translator must act as an L_1 reader and uncover all of the semantic relations between heading and L_1 text. He must recreate those semantic relations in the L_2 text using different linguistic resources. There are several possible solutions in German: *Wahr oder falsch, wenn es nur Sinn gibt* or *Sinnsuche ohne Rücksicht auf Wahrheit*, or even *Sinn um jeden Preis*. The last version is acceptable because it appropriately reflects the relevance relations, not because it is the most literal. Of course, other factors also influence the acceptability of a headline. Relevance is demanded, but a choice among relevant headlines is often made on other grounds. German headlines are generally more explicit than their English counterparts. A journal like *The Times Literary Supplement*, from which this headline was selected, has no stylistic equivalent among German-language publications. The last headline, quite appropriate in many respects, might be rejected on stylistic grounds by L_2 editors.

Maxim of Manner

The concept of relevance leads to Grice's fourth and final maxim. The injunction, in short form, is: *Be perspicuous*. According to Grice, the maxim advises clarity, lack of ambiguity, brevity, and orderliness. Grice uses the term perspicuous in a special way. Clarity, brevity, and orderliness, like relevance, are linked to intentionality. Authors have to be as perspicuous as they need to be, given their communicative intent (personal communication, Grice to R. Beaugrande; Beaurande and Dressler 1981, 120). Authors often have multiple objectives when they communicate. Some of them are obvious. Instruction manuals are meant to instruct. Assembly manuals show their readers how to assemble bicycles, computers, and model airplanes. Political speeches intend to convince, motivate, or dissuade. Jokes and parodies amuse and ridicule. The maxim of manner implies that the textual organization we use should further the goals of our interaction. It may be that one kind of text requires down-to-earth, specific descriptions of processes; another may require the use of veiled threats, ambiguous promises, and circuitous logic.

Actual texts are rarely ideal texts. Even though textual organization may vary by text-type, some empirical texts will always deviate from the norm for their type. It may even be that the statistical (empirical) norm for a type is less than ideal. Early computer software manuals from the seventies were almost all uniformly unreadable and not particularly instructive. Grice's maxim of manner is an exhortation for texts to be organized and structured as effectively and efficiently as they can be, given their purposes. Unfortunately, most texts do not attain Grice's ideal.

How does the maxim of manner affect translation? The maxim raises some difficult issues. First, since source texts may be unclear, ambiguous, verbose, and poorly organized, should the translation correct these failings? The answer to this question depends on two factors: the text type and the intentionality of the text. It seems clear that in certain cases, as in the translation of manuals, the text type and the instructive intent give the translator latitude to follow Grice's maxim and improve the quality of the L_2 text. Any changes or improvements should clearly be improvements and should not violate the essential relevance of the original text. Further, some organizational changes might be demanded because of L_2 textual expectations. German scientific texts are usually more digressive than English scientific texts. Each is acceptable in its own context; in their natural environments these texts are *as perspicuous as they need to be*. The translation of the German text into English, however, might call for the translator to prune the digressions. The translator would need to produce a more direct relevance structure for the text. What a reader takes for brevity, clarity, and organization is culture-specific. For many texts it should be possible to define an *optimal* text. The optimal text may be a normative text. This is a heuristic model constructed from a corpus of actual texts by statistical means. However, the corpus may not yield an optimal text. A random sample of one thousand instruction manuals may not necessarily produce a model of the most effective, comprehensible, and well-organized manual. An optimal text may have to be created by selecting from the corpus all of those features which are typical of the textual category and all of those features which act to enhance the function of the text. Selection of features might be guided by psychological, cognitive, or pedagogical criteria.

If the translator has an optimal text as a guide, and it is clear that the function of the text will be improved with no loss of essential meaning or relevance, then the maxim of manner should be followed. If such heuristic texts are not available, and if the translator violates the intentionality and function of the text by making modifications, he should desist. For instance, in a political speech there may be significance attached to ambiguous statements and a purpose to circuitous logic.

There are cases where L_2 textual expectations make it necessary to modify the textual arrangement of the source text. This can occur even when the source text appears to be ideal. English advertisements are changed dramatically when they are translated into German. Translators who want to create effective advertising copy in another language must do more than translate; they must *co-write*. The text is adapted completely to L_2 textual and cultural requirements. It is not simply recreated. It may even be a new text delivering a similar message (Harris 1983, 129). The manner of presentation is changed entirely, but the intentionality is preserved.

The translating of advertisements, with its "twin bed" marketing technique, may be an extreme example (Bouchard 1960). Most translation restructurings and modifications are more modest and quite selective. The significance of the maxim of manner for the translator is that it calls for a continual assessment of L_2 textual components. The translator must decide whether they carry the L_1 sender's message effectively. There are, however, unanswered questions. How can the translator make a reasonable assessment of potential L_2 textual elements? How can the most effective text be built if the structure of the source text is not always a reliable guide?

Situationality

Grice's four maxims are useful guidelines for the translator. But the principle of cooperation is not enough to produce acceptable translations. Acceptability, receptive intentionality, and cooperation presume that the translator or text producer has imagined a social and pragmatic context for the text-to-be. Texts are always situated in discrete communicative and social settings. The *situationality* of texts is a major component of their textuality. Situationality is the location of a text in a discrete sociocultural context in a real time and place. Recognizing and accounting for situationality is one of the translator's primary responsibilities.

The translator should understand the receptive context of the message he is translating. He should know his communicative partners and their attitudinal state. He should have a grasp of their need for the information in the text, and how they intend to use it. The translator might also want to know something about the social, political, and economic conditions of the receptive speech community. A text producer normally understands the situation in which his text will be activated. In face-to-face conversation the cues for assessing situation are physically present. In written communication the text producer projects a typical receptive situation and constructs a text with that projection in mind. In translation the text is transformed. It will be activated in a situation never intended by the L_1 author.[31] The translator is a mediator who acts simultaneously as an L_1 receiver and an L_2 sender.

Translation allows the knowledge in a text produced for an L_1 situation to be transferred into an L_2 text adapted for an L_2 situation. Situationality is the central issue in translatability. If a translation is to succeed, there must be a situation which requires it. There must be a *translation need*. Many academic examples of so-called "untranslatability" are actually examples of texts for which a receptive situation does not exist. Argument from these examples is a trivial academic exercise. Why should a book on the theory of relativity be translated into the languages of the Australian aborigines? Why should very specific local news items be translated for the international press? Many L_1 texts are highly directed; they refer to localized situation-specific knowledge. Why should this knowledge be transmitted to L_2 users when they have no need, desire for, or interest in that knowledge? As soon as a situation can be envisioned (and there may be a myriad reasons for L_2 users to "need" an L_1 text), then the problem solving process of translation can begin. The need, motivation, or purpose of a translation defines its situationality. The purpose influences the way the translation is carried out. The situationality of the translation is never the same as the situationality of the source text. Situationality is an attribute of the text in its receiver orientation. The translator must be responsible for projecting the situationality of the text-to-be.

Earlier in the volume we mentioned that translation is a problem-solving activity. The translation is a problem waiting to be solved. Problem-solving presupposes that there is a goal state for the process to achieve. Texts are directed at particular receptive partners; translation must also be directed. Once the goal state is defined, the translator can select the strategies that will be used to achieve the goal state. The motivation for a translation shapes the translation process decisively. Beaugrande and Dressler's term *situation management*, which they use to refer to monolingual discourse, can be applied to the translator's mediating effort to orient the text to the text receiver's goals (Beaugrande and Dressler 1981, 168). Situation management is a dynamic monitoring of the translation which guides it toward the receiver and his or her needs. It is a specific form of problem-solving. The situationality of a text can be conceived of as a set of pragmatic parameters which are taken into account by the text producer or translator using a projection of the receptive situation. The management of situation is the factoring of these projected pragmatic parameters into the text production process.

When a professional translator begins a translation, he or she relies on previous experience with similar texts and similar receptive situations. There are empirical clusters of textual situations distributed throughout a communicative community. Each of these clusters exhibits characteristic features. Some of these textual situations are well understood and may even be codified. They are discrete *situation types*. For instance, the translation of patents is a very specific skill. Even though there may be an infinite variety of things patented, the experienced translator understands that the situations in which patents are used are quite limited and very normative. There are only a limited number of social roles (patent lawyer, design engineer) concerned with patents and a limited number of social situations in which the texts are used. This extremely normative situation has been codified in a basic international patent structure (Lawson 1983). Translators can use the patent structure to guide their translations of English, French, or German patents. Patent translation illustrates the concept of situation type.[32] Situation types are routinized situations. Because of their normative character, patent translations are treated as legal documents in international patent conventions. Specialists regularly consult patent translations; they have no need to consult the original source patents. Standardization has reduced the complexity of the translator's problem-solving. Standardization is possible because there is a complete understanding of the purposes of the texts, the needs and backgrounds of their respective users, and the kinds of information to be transmitted. The definition of standard textual types is only possible if the situationality of the text has been fully understood by the standardizing bodies. Standardization allows the translator to produce fully legitimate L_2 texts. Their acceptability and relevance are ensured (Beaugrande and Dressler 1981, 179).[33] This easy legitimacy is not typical of most translations.

Many texts have a common situationality. This may cross cultural and linguistic boundaries. Some of the texts share situationality because of international standardization. Others have developed a *de facto* consensus-based standardization. The majority of the scientific and technical literature falls into this category. Other texts, such as political tracts and newspaper editorials, share fewer common features across cultural boundaries. For these texts, differences in ideology, value system, class structure, and gender identification may make it very difficult for the translator to manage the situation during translation. Translation is always easier when the situation of the L_1 text parallels the situation of the L_2 text. In these cases, the situation can be said to already exist in the L_2 culture. The general strategy of the translator is to adjust the text to its new situation. Adjustments may involve a variety of translation procedures, including explicitation, compression, recasting, and textual re-arrangement. This list is by no means exhaustive. These modifications are not an unwarranted tinkering with the text. The modifications are motivated by the need to preserve the intentionality and functionality of the text in its new situation. This motivation can apply to literary as well as technical texts.

Candace Séguinot conducted a study of situational modifications required in the English versions of journalistic texts reprinted from *Le Monde* (Séguinot 1982). In her examination of these texts, which appeared in *The Guardian Weekly*, the author was explicit in saying that she was not interested in "those differences which emanated from the propensity of one language to express a given idea in a particular linguistic form" (Séguinot 1982, 152).

Her objective was to investigate those differences which "clearly arose from a change in the communicative situation" (Séguinot 1982, 153). *Le Monde* caters primarily to French intellectuals. It is a national newspaper with domestic interests. *The Guardian Weekly* reprints articles from *Le Monde* and from a number of other sources, including the British *Guardian* and the American *Washington Post*. It is directed to a predominantly international readership of English-speaking diplomats, businessmen, and other literate travelers. In her examination of ten *Le Monde* articles which appeared in *The Guardian Weekly* during October and November of 1981, Séguinot described 175 differences between the source and target versions of the texts (Séguinot 1982, 159). In all cases the modifications were situational adaptations of the L_2 text aimed at making textual information more accessible to L_2 readers. The following is a functional categorization of the modifications:

1. changes to improve readability or explicitness: 50 percent

2. adaptations to the target audience: 21 percent

3. reductions in emotive and figurative language: 21 percent

4. alterations to increase objectivity: 4 percent

5. reductions in journalistic style: 4 percent

Situational adaptation of a target text is a complex issue for the translator. The translator is clearly required to adapt the text to its target situation, but his or her knowledge of the target situation is often limited. Instead of informed decision-making, there is sometimes nothing more than intelligent guessing. Nevertheless, although we are far from an objective understanding of which modifications are necessary, and which are not, the concept of situationality remains a central focus for the translator. Situationality keeps translators from presuming that the source text provides everything that they need to know. It keeps them from taking the L_2 reader for granted.[34]

Translation scholars should take on the job of investigating situationality in a rigorous way. Empirical studies, such as the one just described, can help to define the scope and general character of the modifications that are required when specific L_1 and L_2 situations are paired. These studies are likely to reveal that there is a fine line between translation and adaptive editing. For many kinds of texts, particularly legal, commercial, and technical texts, rules of *situational equivalence* (in the isomorphic sense) might be developed. These would resemble the rules we accept for making the transpositions required by systemic differences in language pairs.

INFORMATIVITY

Situationality, intentionality, and acceptability are three of the determining features of textuality. They are, by extension, three of the defining variables of translation. The fourth feature of textuality is *informativity.* A communication situation is a context where information transfer occurs. We say that texts are informative if they provide a knowledge or understanding which did not exist before. If a text tells us nothing new, its information content is low. Informativity in the translation process is a measure of the information a translation provides to an L_2 reader about L_1 events, states, processes, objects, individuals, places and institutions. The original information source was an L_1 text intended for an L_1 audience. Translation opens an *information channel* between senders and receivers who could not normally inform one another about their respective states of affairs. There is a close relationship between situationality and informativity. L_1 and L_2 texts that possess similar situationality will often be similarly informative. They will carry the same kinds of knowledge to their respective readers. Situationality determines the need for information. Situation determines the content that must be transferred. A woman assembling a bicycle in Saxony and a man assembling a bicycle in Ohio share a common situation. The situation conditions their need for information and dictates the mode of its delivery. This is not to say that the mode of delivery will be the same in both cases, since cultural variation is an aspect of situation.

Texts exist in the L_2 culture whose situationality and informativity are similar to that of the translation. If the informativity of L_1 and L_2 texts are identical, there is no need for translation. The existing L_2 text serves the same purpose a translation would serve. Common situationality and *similar* informativity define so-called *parallel texts.* These are L_2 and L_1 texts of similar informativity which are used in more or less identical communicative situations.[35] True parallel texts are not the results of previous translation. They are results of a process of parallel evolution. They spring from similar cultural needs to serve congruent interests in comparable situations. In America there are legal contracts, patents, business letters, theater programs, and computer manuals. In Germany, France, and China, these same kinds of texts exist in the same kinds of situations.

Parallel texts are one of the translator's most important tools. They can provide direct guidance in the construction of the target text. Parallel texts should exhibit most of the features that the translation should possess. They are *native texts,* original inhabitants of the text world of the target culture, and represent an ideal to which the translation should aspire. A good translation may become a kind of parallel text. If the mimicry is complete, and if the text produced is indistinguishable from a native text, then the translation has passed the linguistic equivalent of the computer scientist's Turing Test.

The translator should be critical in the selection of parallel texts. The collection of parallel texts is an important part of translation practice. The uncritical collection of texts might lead the translator to use bad examples. The fact that a text is parallel to one's intended translation does not mean that all parallel texts are created equal. The parallel texts accepted for the translator's working collection should be optimal examples. How can a translator be guided in this selection? There are style-books and writing manuals for many kinds of texts. They specify features of style, syntax, organization, and situation. Translators should use the advice given in these handbooks to evaluate the parallel texts they have collected. These stylistic resources may also be used as *special heuristic texts* in their own right (Shreve 1992).

The informativity of a text is tied to the pattern of semantic relationships expressed by its linguistic surface. Informativity is a function of *what* is delivered by the text; it is a function of its substantive knowledge content. The translator's commission is to create a linguistic surface that will allow the L_2 user to retrieve from the text the same knowledge content that was in the L_1 original.[36] This is a complicated task; the text processing of information structures through linguistic expressions promises to be one of the most difficult and resistant areas of translation research.[37] The translator tries to create conditions which will allow the L_2 user to retrieve the knowledge encoded in a translated text. These conditions can be difficult to achieve when a text has no analogue in the L_2 community. Parallel texts do not exist if there is no equivalent textual situation. Even if a translator is well versed in the social, cultural, and ideological background of the L_1 communicative community, it will be difficult for him or her to transfer the knowledge contained in the text. It is difficult to compensate for the fact that the L_2 community has no experience with the kind of text being translated.

Translation alters and redistributes the orders of informativity of a text (Beaugrande and Dressler 1981, 141–146). This is not just a matter of rearranging surface elements because of linguistic difference. Redistribution is required by the influence of divergent framing systems on the retrieval process. The translator cannot always be sure about the conclusions an L_2 reader will draw from what is heard or read. A text segment with a very low order of informativity in the original might be of a very high order in the L_2 version. What is relevant in one text might be considered trivial in the other. The *order of informativity* is a measure of the *significance* of the information units in a text. This measure is relative to the other information items in the text. It is to be distinguished from relevance, which is a measure of the importance of the information to the reader. A translator may waste a lot of effort to transfer a piece of information to the target text if its importance goes unrecognized. The translator can sometimes deal with this problem (if the difference in mutual knowledge is not too great) by using textual devices to direct the L_2 user's attention to ideas from the L_1 text which should be relevant in the L_2 situation. This strategy cannot resolve the issue completely. Often the L_2 reader simply does not have the background necessary to recognize the significance of what is being read or heard. He or she may be an average or lay reader of a specialized text.[38] The network of associations embedded in the L_1 text which are transferred to the L_2 text cannot be reassembled. Reconstruction is blocked because the L_2 user cannot recognize the elements of the network and their relations. The translator may have to intervene by inserting footnotes, providing translator's notes, or creating explanatory paraphrases. The translator is trying to bring the L_2 reader to an informational threshold by providing extra information. Informativity is not just a function of transferring information already in a text. Ideally, the translator's intervention is hidden from the reader. The translator may have deleted unintelligible and therefore unknowable segments of the L_1 text. Paraphrases, if knitted seamlessly into the text, will be invisible.

Sometimes information transfer in a translation is blocked at the linguistic surface. Lexical items may not have familiar equivalents in the L_2. Equivalents may exist, but they are attached to their knowledge frames quite differently. Consider this article from a British daily and the translation problems which arise in its translation for German newspaper readers (*Morning Star*, 20 September 1983):

> Row mars Gavaskar Test hundred
>
> Indian opener Sunil Gavaskar moved within one century of Sir Donald Bradman's world Test record of 29 hundreds as the first Test against Pakistan finished on a sour note yesterday.
>
> Gavaskar hit an unbeaten 103 in an unbroken first wicket stand of 176 with Anshuman Geakwad before the game ended in a predictable draw.
>
> It was the prospect of Gavaskar scoring his 28th Test century which led to controversy. At the end of the 14th over of the mandatory 20 in the final hour, Gavaskar was 87 not out and Pakistan captain Zaheer Abbas led his team off the field . . .

> Eventually, the Pakistan team trooped out to play the remaining six overs and it was from the first ball of the final over that Gavaskar reached his hundred...
>
> It was only after 10 overs of the final 20 overs had been bowled that Gavaskar made any serious efforts to get his century before time ran out. He was 64 not out at this point...

The translator can provide German equivalents for most of the English terms:

1. Test hundred: *hundert Läufe in einem internationalen (Kricket) Vergleichskampf*

2. opener: *erster Schlagmann*

3. century: *hundert (oder mehr) Läufe*

4. hit an unbeaten 103: *unangefochten 103 Läufe, d.h. Punkte machen*

5. an unbroken first wicket stand: *Nichtausscheiden des zweiten Schlagmanns am Dreistab, d.h. am Kricketmal*

6. over: *Satz von 6 Bällen*

7. mandatory 20: *20 Pflichtsätze*

8. 87 not out: *87 Läufe/Punkte ohne ausgeschieden zu sein*

Linking esoteric cricket terms with more mundane German constructions would produce a fairly intelligible German text. The average L_2 reader might also get an inkling of the main point of interest, the Indian cricketer approaching a world record. But many of the relevant details will be lost to him. A translation of the last paragraph demonstrates the point:

> Erst nachdem 10 der letzten 20 Sätze gespielt waren, unternahm Gavaskar ernsthafte Anstrengungen, vor Ablauf der Zeit seine Hundert zu erreichen. Zu diesem Zeitpunkt hatte er es auf 64 gebracht.

A typical German reader will wonder how this situation could occur and might simply consider most of the last paragraph inexplicable. One might argue that this is not a problem of translation but a problem of mutual knowledge. Of course, assessment of mutual knowledge is one of the translator's major obligations. The translator must make assumptions about what his audience knows. Somewhere there may be a German reader who has studied the rules of cricket and is an expert on openers and Test matches. However, given the fact that the text is a newspaper article, most of the audience for the L_2 text will be unfamiliar with cricket and its cultural background. The L_2 audience's knowledge deficit is a translation problem. The translator, space permitting, could provide additional information. The translator could tell the L_2 readers where and when Sir Donald Bradman scored his twenty-nine hundreds; the translator might indicate the significance of this feat in the overall context of cricket competitions. Still, the informativity of the L_2 text is often an approximation of the informativity of the L_1 text. When the information conveyed in an L_1 text overloads the L_2 user's processing resources, the translator has to contextualize unexpected items or replace them with more familiar elements. Such a procedure is not limited to the search for difficult words and phrases, like using *Internationaler Kricket-Vergleichskampf zwischen Ländern des Britischen Commonwealth* for *Test match*. It also involves making the informativity relations within the text more explicit. Using the rendering *Am Ende fehlte dem Inder Gavaskar noch ein Hunderter von den historischen 29 Hunderten, die der Australier Sir Donald Bradman 1930 erzielt hatte* as a translation for the last sentence activates a reference to the opening paragraph. It underscores the major theme of the article for the L_2 reader and gives a semantic continuity to the translation.

COHERENCE

Modifications in the semantic structure of the text involve the fifth determinant of textuality, *coherence*. The information contents of a text are not randomly transmitted semantic quanta. Grice's maxims of manner and relation tell us that there is order imposed on the information content. This order is a logical structure which defines the semantic connections between information units in the text (Beaugrande and Dressler 1981, 84). Coherence is a property which texts assume when their information contents take on such a logical structure. Coherence can also be seen as a property of the associational structure created by linguistic copresence. Text-based translation attempts to re-establish in the target text a coherence functionally parallel to that of the source text. A translator cannot usually re-establish coherence using literal sentence-for-sentence renderings. L_2 coherence must be recreated using the translator's understanding of the coherence structure of the original to direct modifications in the L_2 textual surface.

In the text *Row mars Gavaskar Test hundred*, the coherence structure is quite transparent, even to readers without an in-depth knowledge of cricket. Assuming that readers are led to invoke a generalized *ball game* frame where success is dependent on the ability to score, a coherence chain can be established by tracing the progression of the score. A logical structure for the text can be derived by a combination of temporal relations (the progression of the cricket match) and references to the score at particular points in the progression. For instance, a declaration in the first paragraph, *Gavaskar moved within one century . . . of 29 hundreds (Gavaskar kam fast an das 29. Hundert heran)*, is actually a reference to the final outcome of the match. The statement expresses the major theme of the text. In the second paragraph there is a specification of this declaration, *Gavaskar hit an unbeaten 103 . . .* , that elaborates on the total score at the end of the game. The third paragraph moves from the end of the match (whose outcome is now known by the reader) to a point within the match, *the prospect of Gavaskar scoring his 28th Test century (Gavaskar war drauf und dran, sein 28. Hundert vollzumachen)*. The progress of the game is indicated by another specification: *the end of the 14th over of the mandatory 20 . . . in the final hour (am Ende des 14. Satzes der regularen 20 Sätze . . . der letzten Stunde)*. At this point, the progress of the score is referenced, *Gavaskar was 87 not out (Gavaskar hatte bereits 87 Punkte gesammelt)*. Then the author introduces one of the main themes mentioned in the headline, the *row* or argument which *mars Gavaskar Test hundred*. After four paragraphs (omitted in our example), the coherence chain is taken up again: *Eventually the Pakistan team trooped out to play the remaining six overs (die ausstehenden sechs Sätze)*. The phrase *remaining six overs* refers back to an earlier temporal sequence, *14th over of the mandatory 20*, when the game was interrupted. The next clause, *and it was from the first ball of the final over that Gavaskar reached his hundred (mit dem ersten Ball im letzten Satz erzielte er seine hundert Läufe)*, marks the progression of the game (in the final or 20th over) and picks up a thematic reference from the first paragraph. The phrase *reached his hundred* is a reference to the 28th hundred introduced as a relevant topic in paragraph one: *Gavaskar moved within one century . . . of 29 hundreds*.

A coherent text has an underlying logical structure that acts to guide the reader through the text. This structure helps the reader overcome his ignorance of specific details. Consider the analogy of a pilot entering a new harbor. He or she may be ignorant of the exact location of shoals, sandbars, or hidden rocks, but there are navigational devices, buoys, and lights which assist the ship into port. The connections between important textual elements should be distinct enough to attract and guide the L_2 reader's attention. The coherence pattern traces the thread of a consistent information structure. It should support the informativity and intentionality of the text. The text producer and the translator use an inventory of textual and linguistic devices to draw attention to the information structure they want the reader to recognize and retrieve. They do this to support the L_2 reader in the construction of a mental model of the text. Johnson-Laird has said of monolingual communication that "subjects interpret sentences by constructing mental models in which the relevant events and entities are represented" (Johnson-Laird 1981, 124). The translator must use the linguistic and textual resources of the target community to re-establish in the L_2 text the potential for an L_2 reader to assemble a mental model. This model may be similar (though probably not identical) to the mental model constructed by an L_1 reader of the text if the situationality of the text is identical.

Coherence, as a mechanism for linking concepts, imparts to words and constructions more meaning than they contain in isolation. It reduces, at the same time, the number of alternate meanings that might be attached to those elements. Procedural semanticists have argued that meanings are not static. Meaning is constructed, emerging as the result of processes applied when texts are read or heard. According to Woods, "human communication relies in a critical way on an ability of the receiver to deduce a much more precise understanding of the intended meaning of an utterance than is conveyed by the words alone and the syntactic structure in which they are incorporated" (Woods 1981, 305). There is a balance between representation and process, between the mental image evoked by a lexical construction and its transformation within the textual environment. It is not possible to isolate the investigation of mental representations from the processes that manipulate them (Johnson-Laird 1981, 118).

Determiners of Coherence

Given our discussion of coherence, it remains to examine the mechanisms that produce it. What are the textual and linguistic agents that connect concepts and allow a translator to create a logical framework for the text (Beaugrande 1980, 19)? The raw materials of coherence are supplied when a text producer embeds elements of his or her stock of knowledge in the text. More raw material is supplied when the text user applies a stock of knowledge to the interpretation of the text. But coherence is not an information unit; it is the connection of individual information elements to create larger, more global structures of meaning. A specific configuration and progression of knowledge elements are created within the text. A person who reads a text can only bring knowledge of events, actions, objects, and situations to bear if those discrete elements are presented as part of a larger pattern. This larger pattern may be seen as a propositional structure which places the elements (actions, objects, events) of the knowledge domain in logical relation to one another. Underlying an utterance is a proposition and underlying a text is an arrangement of propositions. It is this underlying global arrangement that the translator will reproduce in the target text. Coherence is not the propositional structure itself. Coherence is the property that texts take on when they have an underlying (and consistent) propositional structure.

In the cricket text discussed earlier, temporal relationships and partitive relationships play an important part in building a global propositional arrangement. The meaning of each individual utterance is related to other utterances using linguistic devices. Lexical items and linguistic constructions are chosen because they fit the requirements set by the underlying framework. Witness the partitive conceptual connections implied by the following clauses: *At the end of the 14th over of the mandatory 20, the Pakistan team trooped out to play the remaining six overs,* and *it was only after 10 overs of the final 20 overs.* Underlying these statements is a propositional structure; an "over" is part of the game of cricket and twenty overs make a game. This proposition is not explicitly stated, but it is linguistically represented. Likewise, *Gavaskar moved within one century, Gavaskar hit an unbeaten 103, Gavaskar was 87 not out,* and *He was 64 not out at this point* establish partitive relationships. The proposition underlying these structures is: a century is composed of 100 points, scoring is in the form of points, centuries are units of the test match record. Temporal relationships are linked to the progression of the overs: *At the end of the 14th, the remaining six overs, after 10 overs.* The linguistic resources used are selected to convey the underlying ideational structure of the text; they, in turn, serve to create that structure in the mind of the reader. The implication is that ideational structure is conceived first, and then resources are chosen to express it. The conclusion for translation is that the ideational structure has to be understood by the translator before target language resources can be chosen to recreate it.

English newspaper articles typically establish a basis for coherence by clustering information in a lead paragraph. The primary topical elements are specified in the lead paragraph; the actors (Sunil Gavaskar, team Pakistan), the main action (moving within one century of Bradman's record), and the main object (the Test record) are all placed in relation to one another. Time and situation are specified. Everything that follows in the text refers back to this basic information. A translation error, *Gavaskar setzte alles auf eine Karte, um seine hundert zu erreichen, aber die Zeit war um,* implies that Gavaskar tried to get his century but time ran out. This error would violate the coherence structure established in the lead paragraph and make the whole piece incoherent. The effects of mistakes in translation are rarely restricted to the items or sentences where they are committed. They have repercussions within the text because coherence relations connect the damaged item to other items. If the coherence role of the mistranslation is minimal, the global effect of the mistake might be very weak. A mistake in translating the lead paragraph, however, might have disastrous effects. The lead paragraph is the propositional anchor for the text.

Beaugrande provides an interesting example of how mistranslations can destroy the coherence of literary works. He uses Leishman's translation of two lines from Rilke's *Der Panther* (Beaugrande 1980b).

> His glance, so tired from traversing his cage's
> repeated railing, can hold nothing more
>
> Sein Plick ist vom Vorübergehn der Stäbe
> so müd geworden, daß er nichts mehr hält.

The problem here is that in the German original it is the motion of the *bars* which causes the weariness of the panther's gaze. It is the state of weariness that causes his glance "to hold nothing more." The opening connects with the following lines and with the whole stanza. The mistranslation reverberates as the poetic text evolves:

> Ihm ist, als ob es tausend Stäbe gäbe
> und hinter tausend Stäben keine Welt.

Leishman's translation does not retain the coherence of the original. In the opening lines, the main image, the movement of the bars, is replaced by the more literal and trivial movement of the panther's eyes. As a result, the next two lines go astray:

> He feels as though there were a thousand cages,
> and no more world thereafter than before.

Beaugrande's own version retains the coherence of the original by maintaining the conceptual connections (Beaugrande 1980b, 33).

> The passing of the bars has made his gaze
> so weary it no longer can contain.
>
> It seems to him a thousand bars remain;
> beyond the bars the world no longer stays.[39]

There is no doubt that understanding the factors that determine coherence in the L_1 text is an important factor in translation. The translator's own mental model of the text guides him when he selects linguistic resources for his rendering of the L_2 text. The concept of coherence also makes it possible to develop a program for translation criticism. The maintenance of coherence could be established as a criterion for adequate translation.

Typology of Coherence Markers

Is it possible to generalize the mechanisms that are used to establish coherence and thereby generate a useful translation tool? The success of such a venture is linked to the difference between informativity and coherence. Informativity is the specific information content of the text, and coherence is the textual expression of an abstract logical structure linking elements of that content. The difficulty is that there is no clear demarcation between the content of a text and its logical organization. Any analysis which leaves the specifics of content behind will yield abstract logical calculi without the rules of application necessary to tell us how to use them. Alternatively, if one remains too close to the specific content, there are no useful generalizations to be made (or taught) about how coherence is established.

Conceptual dependency theory (Schank 1975; Schank and Abelson 1977) was a useful early attempt to reach the middle ground between abstract calculus and content-specific representation. Its aim was to reduce the complexity of the content, the specific meanings of sentences and texts, to a relatively small number of primitives.[40] These primitives (primarily action-based) are used with names for actors, objects, directions, instruments, states, and values to represent the conceptual frameworks of sentences. There are two kinds of frameworks: *active* and *passive*. The active is expressed as *Actor Action Object Direction (Instrument)* and the passive as *Object (is in) State (with value)*. For example, if ATTEND is a primitive representing the act of attending or of orienting one's senses to a stimulus, then the underlying framework of *John Listens* might be *John ATTEND ear*. Similarly, *John ATTEND eye to Jane* could represent *John sees Jane*. Schank's actual formulations are more complex; the primitive MTRANS (referring to the transfer of mental information between subjects) is interpolated, and ATTEND is treated as the instrument of MTRANS. Further, since a mental act requires a conscious processor, Cp (a place where something is thought of), and a long term memory, LTM (where things are stored), the framework might be better expressed as: *John MTRANS (picture) to Cp (John) from Jane; inst (John ATTEND eyes to Jane)*. Conceptual dependency theory does provide for reducing the range of representations needed to describe the logical structure of most sentences, but there are difficulties.

In real life there are few actions, properties, or attributes that are simply present or not present. For instance, in the sentence *John killed Mary*, let us reduce Mary's condition (of being dead) to some more general state called HEALTH. If we do this, we need some way to express distinctions among other states in the HEALTH domain: dead, diseased, ill, well, healthy. We might represent dead as -10 and extremely healthy as $+10$ on some sort of HEALTH scale. There will be as many intervals on the scale as there are naturally occurring concepts of health in the cultural stock of knowledge.

Conceptual dependency theory illustrates the kind of problems that an attempt to develop a typology of coherence mechanisms will involve. There must be a mechanism for reduction. This will allow generalizations about coherence patterns present in a broad corpus of texts. There must be a mechanism for representation. This will allow us to express the common features of coherence structures in the corpus. At best, dependency theory will yield a limited typology. It will be able to characterize the sense relations in very simple texts dealing with everyday events in the physical world. Schank is aware of the limitations when he admits, "what we have had in conceptual dependency is a system for describing the physical world. Scripts, plans, and goals allowed us to look at the intentions and knowledge behind these physical events" (Schank and Carbonell 1979, 328).

Beaugrande's typology of concepts and relations is a similar attempt at the textual level (Beaugrande 1980a, 78–86). It has reductive power but is also capable of expressing the diversity of coherence mechanisms that occurs in texts. The system assumes that any text focuses on the representation of one or more *primary concepts*. The primary concepts may be events, actions, objects, or situations.[41] These elemental concepts are linked to a more elaborate set of modifying concepts called *secondary concepts*. Secondary concepts supply information about primary concepts; they specify properties, states of being, locations, orientations, and time relations. A single primary concept could not possibly underlie a text. Something has to be said about the concept.[42] It is not clear whether any typology of coherence markers or system of coherence representation will be of use in practice. Translation theorists have to be careful when they propose elaborate schemes which no practicing translator can use or would have the time to use. A more useful approach would be to extrapolate systems such as Beaugrande's and develop teaching materials from them. These materials could illustrate typical patterns of coherence. By teaching translation students about coherence and its creation, we ensure that they will be able to produce coherence in the real texts that will form their life's work.

Global Coherence

The translator uses instances of the L_1 grammatical and lexical system as signposts. Surface features of the text mark primary and secondary concepts and indicate relevant relations between the concepts. The linguistic markers must be translated in such a way that their role in establishing coherence is preserved. However, grammatical and lexical choices in the L_2 text must function independently in the new text. Coherence involves the whole text. Linguistic choices are a reflection of the global coherence pattern. Translation is not a simple matter of taking L_1 sense relations and matching them with L_2 constructions. Coherence is not imported from the L_1 text; coherence is constructed anew in the L_2 text using L_1 sense relations as a template.[43] When L_2 words are selected as possible equivalents, they often bring with them unwanted attachments or implications. These side-effects may have to be minimized and diverted. The following example has a coherence structure based upon a metaphor:

> "Refocusing up-stream" has become a catch-phrase with people involved in health politics, and the reason for its popularity is as follows: A complacent view of health care may see the health services as pulling drowning people out of a river. It may raise questions about who does the saving, or how they do it and who among those to be saved should take priority. Looking "up-stream" however raises the question of how people fell into the water in the first place. Did they fall or were they pushed? The orthodox view . . . is that we fall into the water of our own accord. (*Comment*, 1 September 1979)

A good translation has to account for the use of the expanded metaphor as a global coherence mechanism. There are two basic concepts: prophylactic health care and the images of drowning and rescue. The health care concept structure is organized by the metaphors. The L_1 reader is guided to interpret everything through the filter of the metaphors. The coherence function is signaled by the phrase *may see the health services as pulling drowning people out of a river* and is continued with references to *saving, falling into the water,* and *being pushed into the water.*

The translator has several strategies available. He or she may decide to use the original coherence framework and apply an identical imagery in the second paragraph of the L_2:

> Für alle diejenigen leistet der Gesundheitsschutz genug, die in den Einrichtungen des Gesundheitsschutzes nicht mehr als eine Rettungsanstalt für Ertrinkende aus einem Fluß sehen. Sie fragen danach, wer die Rettung ausführt, wie sie erfolgen und wer zuerst gerettet werden soll. Wer dagegen die Blicke flußaufwärts richtet, der stellt die Frage, warum die Menschen überhaupt erst hineinfallen konnten. Fielen sie oder wurden sie hineingestoßen? Immer hat man geglaubt, . . . wir würden von selbst ins Wasser fallen.

This rendering is appropriate. But what about the catch-phrase in the first paragraph? What does the translator do with the catch-phrase *Refocusing up-stream*? If the translator uses a rendering such as *Den Blick flußaufwärts richten* at the beginning of the first paragraph, there would be coherence with a similar expression in the second paragraph. However, this expression does not function as a catch-phrase in the L_2. The translator could use the equivalent L_2 expression *Vorbeugen ist besser als Heilen* and then continue the paragraph as follows: *. . . ist zum Schlagwort für alle geworden, die mit Gesundheitspolitik zu tun haben. Der Grund für seine Popularität liegt im folgenden.* However, this sequence would violate the coherence of the text. The second paragraph of the L_2 text could not possibly explain the popularity of the L_2 phrase *Vorbeugen ist besser als Heilen*. Should the translator coin a new catch-phrase that will recapture this lost coherence, as in *Nicht erst ins Wasser fallen lassen* or *Vorher das Ufer beobachten / im Auge behalten*? Should the translator sacrifice the image and de-metaphorize the text?

The translator could sever the metaphorical ties connecting the two sub-texts and use the current L_2 catch-phrase *Vorbeugen ist besser als Heilen*. This would entail deleting the secondary concept *reason for its popularity*. The translator might also modify the secondary concept, as in *ist zum populären/weit verbreiteten Schlagwort geworden*. In addition, the iterated phrase *looking up-stream* in the second subtext has to be replaced by *Wer dagegen die Vorbeugung in den Mittelpunkt stellt*. This restores coherence using non-metaphorical means. The last solution turns out to be the most appropriate one.

Cohesion

Coherence and the surface arrangement of lexical structures are clearly interdependent. The projected coherence pattern constrains the lexical choices the translator can make. These constraints do not entail a slavish reproduction of the L_1 pattern. Indeed, an author or translator may have to significantly change the coherence pattern. In any case, a coherence pattern must exist whether it is modeled on the L_1 or created anew. Situational variables and the lexical resources of the target language may force the translator to create another functional coherence pattern. Ultimately, the experienced textual surface must reflect some underlying coherence. The reflection of semantic coherence at the textual surface is the sixth determinant of textuality, *cohesion*.

Of the seven factors that determine textuality, cohesion is the most palpably linguistic. Coherence is a property of the underlying meaning structure of a text; cohesion is a property of the linguistic surface of the text. Cohesion makes coherence linguistically evident. The cohesive text is, as a result, the end product of translation. It is not possible to consider coherence and cohesion separately. The complex interdependence between cohesion and coherence can lead to confusion, even among analysts. Halliday and Hasan use the term *cohesion* exclusively (Halliday and Hasan 1976; Hasan 1968). The concept of coherence is unnecessary if cohesion is defined as a semantic concept which "refers to relations of meaning that exist within the text, and that define it as a text . . . cohesion is part of the system of language" (Halliday and Hasan 1976, 4–5). The authors are primarily interested in exploring the linguistic potential for the expression of semantic relations. They focus on the "systematic resources . . . that are built into the language itself" (Halliday and Hasan 1976, 5). The conceptual frameworks that establish coherence are treated entirely in terms of their linguistic manifestation in texts. The linguistic elements that occur in sequences of sentences act together to form *texture*, a term which refers to cohesive ties at the level of connected discourse (as opposed to cohesive ties within individual sentences). If a text consists of a single sentence, as in the case of inscriptions, slogans, public notices, commands, exclamations, proverbs, quotations, or aphorisms, then texture may be congruent with linguistic structure. This congruence is purely formal.

The one-sentence text, *No smoking*, could be structurally translated as *Kein Rauchen*. But the texture of the sign would not be preserved. The L_2 sentence, which is perfectly well-formed in the L_2 structural system, has to be replaced by *Rauchen verboten* or by *Rauchen nicht erwünscht*, depending on the context. *Kein Rauchen* has structure, but not texture. It violates the acceptability standards for this text in the L_2. Acceptability standards override structural rules; they select certain structural options over others.

Translators can benefit from a distinction between the concepts of cohesion and coherence. Unlike Halliday and Hasan, we propose that cohesion refer only to the expression of conceptual structure through linguistic means. The argument for this distinction is based on the empirical observation of real target texts. Structure-for-structure renderings of the L_1 textual surface which retain L_1 cohesion patterns using L_2 linguistic resources rarely result in effective texts. The translator has to draw upon detailed knowledge of the intricate system of cohesion mechanisms available in the L_2 in order to give appropriate texture to the L_2 text. The texture of the L_1 does not provide any direct guidance for the translator. Dictionaries and contrastive grammars are erratic tools, even if intelligently consulted.

Cohesion is a reflection of the conceptual structure of a particular text; it is also a reflection of the way knowledge is organized. The conceptual structure of the text must be clear in the translator's mind before a cohesive textual surface can be created. An understanding of knowledge structure is critical in technical translation. For instance, the partitive (PART-OF) and generic (IS-A) relationships between machine parts and materials must be expressed in precise linguistic terms. The translator who does not understand the underlying relationships cannot possibly select the correct terms in a translation. There is a meta-linguistic intermediate stage of the translation process that does not exist in a linguistically realized form. At this stage the translator builds a mental model of the text, what we called the *virtual translation* in the first chapter. As soon as this translator realizes this model in the L_2 text, cohesion is governed by the L_2 linguistic system. In other words, once the conceptual structure is chosen, there are only a limited number of language-specific ways to realize it. Cohesion is dependent on coherence, but coherence is also dependent on cohesion. Languages have developed particular devices for establishing cohesion. These mechanisms specify how grammatical and lexical structures can interact at the textual surface.

Cohesion operates across sentence boundaries. Cohesion devices act as orienting signals to connect previously processed (read, heard, stored) items with items yet to be processed. The cohesiveness of the text grows as the text is read. According to Halliday and Hasan (Halliday and Hasan 1976, 4):

> Cohesion occurs where the INTERPRETATION of some element in the discourse is dependent on that of another. The one PRESUPPOSES the other, in the sense that it cannot be effectively decoded except by recourse to it. When this happens, a relation of cohesion is set up, and the two elements, the presupposing and the presupposed, are thereby at least potentially integrated into a text.

The translator's understanding of the cohesion mechanisms operating in the L_1 text must be matched by an understanding of how to create cohesion in the L_2 text using target language resources. The translator should not subject L_2 readers to *cohesion interference*. This condition is caused by the intrusion of L_1 cohesion patterns into L_2 texts. It can also result from the translator's failure to appreciate the cohesion devices active in the L_1 text. These two sources of cohesion interference are not easily distinguished. Some L_1-specific cohesive ties must be "translated away," or they may emerge inappropriately in the L_2 text. Conversely, if L_1 cohesive devices are completely ignored (and the translator does not compensate by establishing an independent but parallel cohesion), the L_2 text may lose its semantic integrity.

Lexical Cohesion

Lexical mistranslations are a common source of cohesion interference because they result in *pseudo-collocations*. These are combinations of L_2 lexical items that are derived from genuine L_1 collocations but do not naturally occur in the target language. Words in the L_1 text occur in sense groups. A sense group derives its character from a conjunction of the semantic features each word brings to the group. Individual word senses can only be decoded by examining their relations to words that come before and after them. There may be local semantic relations among adjacent items in a sense group and there may be global relations between items in more distant parts of the text. Relations between adjacent items create *cohesion by collocation*. Global relations create *word systems*. Both local and global word relationships are based on the lexical semantics of the linguistic system involved. This means that some lexical items, regardless of the particular text in which they occur, are semantically closer to one another than they are to other items. This semantic proximity derives from the linguistic and cognitive systems but is not the same thing as cohesion. Semantic proximity is a culture-bound recognition of the "relatedness" of things. It can provide the basis for cohesion because it directs the potential for establishing actual relations between words in the text. For instance, the names for the primary colors refer to the same knowledge frame. This set of names is a *lexical field*, the linguistic reflection of frame relationships. The names of the colors act cohesively only in conjunction with members of other lexical fields within the textual environment. Thus, *a blue sky, a green meadow*, and *the Emerald Isle* are all phrases whose elements are combinable in texts because of their underlying semantic proximity. The lexical items *sky, meadow*, and *Isle* label concepts which may possess the property of color. *Blue* is a label for a property which objects may possess.

The potential for making collocations derives from the linguistic-semantic system. Problems arise when a translator has to deal with the language-specific ways these combinatory potentials emerge in the text. *Blauer Himmel* and *grüne Wiese* are parallel to equivalent L_1 collocations. *Grüne Insel* is not. This combination is never actualized in German texts even though it may exist as a potential combination. Consider the following sentence from a German travel brochure translated for English-speaking visitors:

> Wenn Sie das Gruseln lernen wollen, dann begeben Sie sich am besten zum Schwarzen Kreuz am Schwarzen Kreuzweg, wo vor vielen Jahren ein Grünrock von einem Schwarzkittel getötet wurde.

Grünrock and *Schwarzkittel* are words whose semantic structure contributes to the imaginative texture of the passage. Notice how the following translation reduces the cohesion of the text:

> If you are out to experience that uncanny feeling one gets at dark crossroads, make your way to the "Black Cross" where many years ago a gamekeeper was killed by a wild boar.

This loss of cohesion might be tolerable in a tourist brochure, but would be unacceptable in poetic translation. Cohesiveness is a matter of degree and can work on various levels. The translation is certainly not without cohesion. The words *gamekeeper* and *wild boar* are semantically related in the English lexicon. *Dark crossroads* is linked to the word *forest* used in a previous paragraph. Nevertheless, it is clear that the L_1 text is more cohesive than the L_2 text. The author has taken pains to invest the linguistic resources necessary to achieve a higher level of cohesion; this investment heightens the effect of the text on the L_1 reader.

Should the translator also invest the effort required to capture the "heightened" texture of the original? The answer depends on the purpose of the text. Because it is a tourist brochure and not a poem, the less cohesive rendering is acceptable. The L_2 text is cohesive enough to express its underlying coherence. The primary concepts and their relationships to the secondary concepts are clear. The translator has chosen to "translate away" the optional cohesive devices and has re-expressed the mandatory ones. This reductive approach is preferable to the use of artificial constructions such as *greencoat* that pretend to recapture the exact cohesion of the original.[44] The example indicates the limits of translation in dealing with lexical cohesion. Consider another passage from this same travel brochure:

> Ein Bummel durch die Stadt erschließt den Besuchern oftmals deutlicher als den Einwohnern selbst das spezifische Leipziger Fluidum, das sich aus der anheimelnden Atmosphäre einer gewachsenen Stadt und den Vorzügen einer modernen Großstadt ergibt. Diese Stadt atmet überall Geschichte. Der Entdeckerfreude des aufmerksamen Beobachters sind keine Grenzen gesetzt.

The collocation *das spezifische Leipziger Fluidum* was rendered as *the specific Leipzig air* in a published version.[45] This token-for-token "dictionary translation" is not an acceptable English rendering. The English word *atmosphere* comes closest to *Fluidum*. If it is used, it would then need to be repeated as an equivalent for *Atmosphäre* later in the text. This is more cohesion than might be desirable. *Aura* is too weak and *air* is too mundane to function as equivalents for *Fluidum*. A translator must also take into account that *Fluidum* is superordinated to both *Atmosphäre* and *Vorzüge*. This superordination creates *hyponymic cohesion*. The verb *sich ergeben* signals the hyponymic relation.

There are no hard and fast rules to guide the translator when he or she tries to recover or create cohesion in the translation. There are no one-to-one equivalents which can be applied by using standard correspondence rules. The translator has several strategies to draw from. Strategies must be selected or discarded depending on the influence of other textual factors. The cohesion of the target text must not violate the primary coherence structure present in the L_1 text. That structure must be essentially re-created in the L_2 text (unless the purpose of the translation dictates otherwise). The translator must not let the freedom to re-create cohesion act against the intentionality and informativity of the text. A translator has to balance cohesion against global textual factors.

Keeping the idea of balance in mind, it could be possible to render the phrase *das spezifische Leipziger Fluidum* as *the sense and character of Leipzig*. This double-headed phrase (*hendiadys*) offers a solution to the problem of choosing an appropriate L_2 collocation for *Fluidum* because it preserves hyponymic cohesion with *the friendly atmosphere of a historical town* and *the amenities of a modern city*.[46] The new word group of *Leipzig, town,* and *city* created by this rendering is cohesive with the hyponymic word group of *sense and character, friendly atmosphere,* and *amenities*.

These cohesive devices serve the underlying coherence structure. The *friendly atmosphere* and the *amenities of a modern city* are reasons for *the sense and character*. There is a logical framework of presupposition and consequence that is actualized by the use of specific cohesive lexical resources. A proper rendering of *sich ergeben* is required to actualize the hyponymic and presuppositional structure. Suitable candidates for expressing the logical relationship are *result from, be the result of, spring from,* or *give rise to*.

Lexical cohesion occurs over a collocational range which crosses clause and sentence boundaries. Lexical choices are interdependent:

> Strolling through the town, visitors will often appreciate, more than a native inhabitant, what gives rise to the sense and character of Leipzig: a combination of the friendly atmosphere of a historical town and the amenities of a modern city.

or

> Strolling through the town, visitors will often get a better idea than a native inhabitant of what makes up the sense and character of Leipzig, the result of a combination of the friendly atmosphere . . .

In the first version, *gives rise to* reflects the presupposition-consequence relation of the underlying proposition. This makes another semantic relation expressed in the form of a *result* verb after *sense and character of Leipzig* redundant. The second version, using *what makes up*, is a weaker indicator of presupposition and consequence. This might recommend the use of *result* in the subordinate clause.

It is clear that choosing one lexical item can affect the use of another. Consider the phrase *Diese Stadt atmet überall Geschichte* which has a partial collocational equivalent in English, *The town breathes history*. Only the sense of *überall* is missing. Using the word *strolling* as a cue, the translator could try the rendering *The town breathes history at every turn*. Another possibility might be to retain the link with *stroll*, but drop the attempt to render *atmet* so literally (even though there is an English equivalent). The rendering *History comes alive at every turn* works just as well and avoids a repetition of the word *town*. The final phrase also illustrates lexical interdependence (*Der Entdeckerfreude des aufmerksamen Beobachters sind keine Grenzen gesetzt*). Because the translation of the first sentence used *visitors*, cohesion can be established in the final sentence by using the word as an equivalent for *Beobachter*. By adding the adjective *attentive*, a major sense attribute of the German noun is preserved. This strategy avoids the use of the English equivalent *observer*, whose sense attributes are out of place in this text. One rendering might be: *The attentive visitor's joy of discovery is unlimited*. If *joy of discovery* appears too trite, then the sense of *joy* can be combined with *attention*, as in *The enthusiastic visitor will be able to make endless discoveries*.

Translation is itself an endless discovery. The translator must select those L_2 items that contribute most effectively to the overall cohesion of the text. He must reject others whose collocational senses contradict it. Translation strategies for establishing cohesion are like game strategies. One decision creates the necessity for another; as the cohesion network grows more complex, some decisions are precluded. The final rendering of the L_2 text is a decision tree.

The travel brochure illustrates some of the lexical mechanisms that can be used to establish cohesion. The basic mechanisms for achieving cohesion are *collocation* and *iteration*. Iteration is the repetition of a word, the use of synonyms and near-synonyms, and substitution by hyponym or superordinate terms (Halliday and Hasan 1976, 288).[47] Iteration is not restricted to lexical items with the same referent. Iteration may also involve words which share the same referent, words which partly share the same referent (as when one word includes the referent of the other), words which exclude each other's referents, or words which are referentially unrelated (Halliday and Hasan 1976, 52).[48] Lexical cohesion is independent of extra-textual referential identity. It operates between text-situated forms. It operates between words that have certain semantic relations with other words in the text. The text determines what belongs together.

Textonymy

The semantic relations established by cohesion are text-bound. The term textonymy refers to the range of word configurations exhibited in texts (Neubert 1979, 22). These configurations can include synonymy, hyponymy, metonymy, metaphor, antonymy, complementarity, converseness, homonymy, gradation, thematic progression, lexical fields, word families, and word systems.[49] Textonymy refers specifically to the transformation of the *paradigmatic* semantic relations in the lexicon into actual *syntagmatic* patterns in the text. A collocation is a textonymic unit, a synthetic complex whose meaning is more than the sum of the "dictionary" meanings of its parts. In the collocation *sense and character*, a complex meaning is created by the near-synonymic iteration of the two words within the text. Collocations are like chemical compounds whose constituent elements have combined to form a new substance with its own properties. Chemical compounds may interact with other compounds to form even more complex substances. Similarly, sets of collocations may be amalgamated into progressively larger and more complex text-cohesive structures. Textonymy is the textual process which creates lexical cohesion by synthesizing progressively larger "chunks" of meaning in the text. These synthetic complexes exist in the L_1 text. The translator exploits the textonymic resources of the L_2 to build similar structures in the target text.

Lexical cohesion typically involves the use of collocations that have been used before. But the full result of textonymy, the texture of the text, may be entirely unique. The discrete textonymic elements of texture may have never been seen in this particular global combination before. However, it is the familiarity of the individual collocations that allows the reader to appreciate its specific textual meaning in this unique global combination.[50]

Word Systems

There is no guarantee that the full texture of the source can be preserved in the translation. Loss of texture occurs because of differences in the linguistic systems and because the translator cannot retrieve all of the meaning indicated by the surface structure. In this respect, the translator is like the L_1 reader. Most readers probably do not retrieve all that has been invested in a text. Semantic attrition is unavoidable. L_2 texture is never identical with L_1 texture because textonymic patterns based on phonological, derivational, connotational, etymological, or folk-etymological relations are destroyed by the process of translation. The textonymic relation that connected *Grünrock* and *Schwarzkittel* in our sample German tourist brochure was destroyed when the translator created an L_2 textonymic relation between *gamekeeper* and *wild boar*.

Some of the relations between words act in direct support of the underlying coherence of the text. Other word relationships may operate at a more indirect level. In their study of Hebrew-English translations, Aphek and Tobin have referred to this secondary set of relations as word systems (Aphek and Tobin, 1981).[51] Word systems are a semantic overlay projecting a second level of semantic relations on the text. This overlay is only indirectly related to the primary logical framework of the text. In literary works, where word systems are most commonly encountered, they ensure that the text is "transformed into a consolidated unit where the message is tightly enclosed within the actual language itself" (Aphek and Tobin 1983, 68).

Some word systems are created intentionally for their aesthetic effect (as in poems or stories). Some are accidental creations. How many of the relationships recognizable in a text were placed there deliberately? Even if they are accidental, word systems can tell us something about an author's personal style; they may reflect influences of class, culture, and gender. Word systems can be a serious problem for the translator. It will usually be impossible to recreate their global textual quality in the L_2 (Aphek and Tobin 1981, 43). Non-literary texts usually have fragmentary word systems, if they have any. Most of these texts (exceptions might include political speeches and editorials) are characterized by a more mundane use of language and a single level of cohesion. For the majority of texts, lexical cohesion is a straightforward pointer to the propositional structure.

Word systems "are polysemic, thus enabling multiple and varied readings of a text" (Aphek and Tobin 1983, 59). As soon as a reader is required to select one of two or more interpretations for a given cohesive relation in the L_1 text, the relation is no longer language independent. The words are no longer arbitrary signs indicating an independent mental content. Translation is in jeopardy whenever words mean too much more than what they say. Allusions are typical examples of polysemic structures with more than one cohesive role.

Such structures are said to exhibit *cohesive polyvalence*. Allusions can occur in pragmatic texts as well as in literary texts. They are not very common in patents and computer manuals but occur regularly in newspaper articles and speeches. Polyvalent structures are like word systems but are more restricted in scope. There is usually only a single structure involved, and it is localized in the text. A translator can usually deal with cohesive polyvalence because of its limited scope.

The phrase *Of mice and men and money* headlines a report about a biomedical research center in the United States where scientists (men) experiment with mice.[52] The scientists finance (money) half of the lab's operating costs by selling two million mice a year. The article summarizes the center's success in organ transplant studies and cancer research. There are a number of straightforward cohesion devices used in the text. *Men* is iterated co-hyponymically: *scientists, geneticists, immunologists, histologists, virologists, cell biologists, embryologists*, the founding director, the present director, a Nobel prize winner, *staff, staff scientists, graduate students, the right man or woman for the job*, and *people involved in cancer research*. *Mice* is repeated thirteen times, and several textonymically related words, such as *strains, colonies, stocks*, and *animals* are used. *Money* is not repeated at all after the headline, but is referenced textonymically in sentences like: *wealthy Americans and their private philanthropy floated the Jackson Laboratory more than fifty years ago*, or *the industrialists who set up and financed the independent Jackson Laboratory*, or *a fund-raising committee keeps an office in the building*. Co-hyponyms like *the lab's income, remaining funds, public grants, private donations, private contribution*, and *private support* are also used.

This direct lexical cohesion can be easily expressed in the L_2 text. However, the headline contains an allusion to John Steinbeck's novel *Of Mice and Men* (in translation: *Von Menschen und Mäusen*). The allusion is an attention grabber which can be traced to a well-known line from Robert Burns's famous poem, *To a Mouse:*

> The best laid schemes o' Mice an' Men
> Gang oft a-gley
>
> Wie oft schlägt fehl der beste Plan
> Bei Mensch und Mäusen.

Steinbeck used this reference to Burns as a symbol of the overpowering forces of nature and their effects on the lives of men and animals.[53] What can the reader of this newspaper article retrieve from the allusion? The reader will not be able to discover a genuine conceptual link between the content of the article and the major themes of Steinbeck's novel. Must the reader take the additional link to Burns's poem into account? Does the translator have to account for the alliteration in the headline, another form of cohesion?

The headline is a typical case of polyvalent cohesion. The translator must evaluate the importance of the allusion by determining the role it plays in helping the reader understand the L_2. Does it contribute to informativity? Does the reference establish coherence? The headline is the logical starting point in the translator's search for textual cohesion. The headline provides three semantic values: *mice, men,* and *money*. These values must be referenced against the body of the text. An evaluation of the relative significance of the three values in the text might allow the translator to make objective choices when it becomes obvious that some semantic loss must occur. It makes no sense to go to great lengths to retain a secondary semantic thread if the essential logic is sacrificed in the attempt. This is not an argument to abandon the allusion. The preservation of the "essential logic" does not imply retaining only those cohesive ties that directly reflect the underlying information structure. If the translator were to pursue only significant information content, then a title such as *Biomedizinisches Forschungszentrum, Erfolge und Finanzierungsprobleme* would suffice. This rendering might be a perfectly legitimate headline for an article directed at an audience of experts in international medical research. The textuality of a newspaper article requires more effort from the translator. He may not be able to retain the specific cohesive character of the original, but he must recapture its functional load, the "eye-catching" impact it has on the reader. Allusions to Steinbeck and Burns should be sacrificed if they cannot play this role in the L_2 text.

If the translator decides that the original allusion cannot be transferred, then the search for creative solutions can begin. Some possibilities might be: *Forschungserfolge und Finanzierungsprobleme,* or *Forschung hilft Menschen, Forschung braucht Mittel,* or perhaps more to the point, *Experimente mit Mäusen kosten Geld.* Literary associations such as *Von Mäusen und Menschen und den nötigen Mitteln* or ... *und dem lieben/leidigen Geld* would probably be inadequate. Most L_2 readers would miss the point.[54] Whatever emerges as the title of the translation must fulfill the same complex cohesive function as the original title. It must inform and somehow grab the attention of the reader. The interactional aims of the L_1 and L_2 headlines are the same even if their surface expression is different.

Grammatical Cohesion

Translation strategies for dealing with problems of lexical cohesion often involve restructuring. Restructuring usually dissolves certain minor L_1 cohesion relations that would be out of place if transferred uncritically. Sometimes truly significant cohesion relations are lost. This can create an *under-translated* L_2 text. Under-translation can be caused by a failure to deal properly with lexical cohesion, but it can also result from a failure to preserve important grammatical and syntactic dependencies. It may seem surprising that grammar plays a role in cohesion. It is easy to assume that grammatical features have no direct impact on the propositional and referential content of a text.

Grammar does more than serve as a structural vehicle for associating words in sentences. Grammatical structures can also serve semantic functions by indicating important relations. However, the cohesive function of grammar is only active within a text. Grammatical cohesion, like lexical cohesion, is a textual phenomenon. A sentence-grammar analysis of a verb phrase describes the morphological and syntactic structure of the phrase and the forms and categories of the verb, including tense, aspect, and mood (Graustein et al. 1977, 98–176). It assigns functions to grammatical structures within the frame of reference of the sentence. In English the grammatical category of aspect is marked morphologically by the contrast between plain and expanded forms. It functions as a linguistic mechanism for indicating the focus of the speaker's interest. The marked member of the categorial pair (with the expanded form of *Verb + ing*) indicates that a process or state (1) is actually progressing or continuing in time, and / or (2) is of limited temporal duration, or (3) is incomplete at a given time.

It is also within subtextual units like the sentence that aspect combines the grammatical categories of tense (present, past, future) and correlation (simultaneity, anteriority, posteriority) (Graustein et al. 1977, 170, 175–176). Explanatory statements such as the first verb phrase in *he was speaking when I joined the banquet* convey the meaning of "action (still) in process, not yet completed." Such a determination can be made without reference to what preceded and what might follow in the discourse. Grammatical structures like these contribute nothing to an understanding of the texture of the larger discourse in which the sentence occurs. The translation *er sprach gerade / hielt (s)eine Rede / war gerade bei seiner Rede, als ich zum Bankett kam / zum Bankett eintraf* can be understood the same way. No textual cues are needed. The absence of morphological aspect markers in German is compensated for by lexical means (adverbs or paraphrases). When translating an individual sentence, it does not matter whether meanings are expressed by grammatical (morphological or syntactic) or by lexical means.

The situation changes if aspectual distinctions are upgraded to provide grammatical cohesion at the textual level. A sequence of sentences containing expanded forms can create the illusion of progression in a group of sentences. At this point, grammatical structure, a property of sentences, becomes texture, a property of texts. It also becomes an issue for the translator. Grammatical structures that operate almost imperceptibly in the L_1 to create cohesion across sentence boundaries can produce incongruities like jarring adverbial chains in the L_2 text. Lexical substitution for grammatical distinctions, a simple transposition strategy that works well at the sentence level, is not as effective when a connected group of sentences is involved. Whenever grammatical features are exploited to provide cohesion over sentence boundaries, there is a high probability that they will be translated away or lexically over-translated.

This includes cases where a grammatical feature used to provide cohesion with adjacent sentences has no counterpart in the L_2. The English verb *say*, which normally does not occur in the expanded form, may be used aspectually if it refers to the acoustic impression of what is said on someone who "is hearing it."[55] In a description of a lively conversation, *X was saying*, or *Y was replying*, or *Z was hearing*, the contrast with the verb in its plain form creates a subtle cohesion pattern combining physical experience (expanded form) and cognitive apperception (plain form). The character of the physical event is reflected in the linguistic description. Using this device in a novel might indicate that the focus alternates between the words said (*X said . . .*) and the act of saying (or hearing) the words said. The author can use this simple grammatical opposition to reflect the alternating perspectives of a narrator or protagonist. Translators working with languages where the same morphological distinction is not made will have a difficult time. They will probably have to create this effect by lexical means.

An example can illustrate some of the issues involved in grammatical cohesion (*Morning Star*, 3 February 1982):

> China's Foreign Minister Wu Xueqian said in Peking yesterday that "further efforts are no doubt necessary to dispel the dark clouds" over Sino-American relations. He was speaking at a ban-

quet for US Secretary of State George Shultz, who arrived from Japan earlier on a five-day visit, which he claimed was aimed at "correcting misunderstandings."

The expanded form in the second sentence (*was speaking*) cannot be interpreted without referring to the preceding paragraph. This structure is often found at the beginning of newspaper articles. At first the facts are stated in the plain form (*said*); then the expanded form is used to contextualize the main idea. This structure is often used if a speech, statement, or remark is quoted in the first sentence or paragraph of the article. The quotation (and the speaker) is usually introduced with the plain form of a "verb of saying" (said, claimed, vowed, denounced) and is followed by the expanded form of the verb.[56]

Consider another example, where the cohesive scope of the expanded form even includes the headline. Such cases often occur when the article is about what someone has said in public (*Morning Star*, 28 December 1982):

> **Thatcher scuppered settlement plan—Dalyell MP vows to dig out the Falkland facts.** Rebel labor MP Tom Dayell yesterday vowed to fight on to find the truth about the Falklands adventure—and made dramatic new charges against Premier Thatcher's conduct of the Falklands war. He claimed that on at least three occasions Mrs. Thatcher ordered military action to scupper a negotiated compromise settlement and therefore caused the unnecessary loss of hundreds of lives. The West Lothian MP was speaking after a Christmas storm of protest over his letter to the Queen begging her to drop phrases backing the war from her Yuletide message.

The L_1 reader tacitly assumes that what preceded *was speaking* is in fact the "mental object" of that verb form. It is re-associated, but not restated. In other words, the expanded form stands for the plain form plus object. The alternative form is sometimes explicitly expressed (*Morning Star*, 31 December 1982):

> **Escaper's boast**
>
> A prisoner on the run, who was re-arrested then mistakenly released by the police, has boasted that he is now leading "the life of Riley." Stephen Sinton, 22, made the claim in an interview in

yesterday's *Birmingham Post*. He also said that he would give himself up in the next fortnight.

Here grammatical cohesion is replaced by a lexical relationship between the verb *claim* and things that were said before. This form of cohesion is rare in English-speaking newspapers. For the translator into German, a language which does not dispose of the aspectual distinction, a rendering of the expanded form by the (simple) preterit *sprach* misses the cohesive relation entirely. A way to avoid the undertranslation would be to follow the model supplied by the L_1 lexical alternative, renderings such as *er traf diese Feststellung/er äußerte diese Ansicht/Behauptung/er vertrat diese Auffassung/er machte diese Bemerkung/Äußerung(en)* or *er äußerte sich in dieser Richtung*. The choice of alternatives depends on the kind of communication that had occurred (plain statement, opinion, claim, assertion, threat). At any rate, the anaphoric function of the expanded form demands a suitable lexical substitution.[57]

The translation of grammatical cohesion in the L_1 by lexical means in the L_2 suggests that it might also be possible to use grammatical renderings in the L_2 for lexical distinctions in the L_1. This actually rarely occurs. L_2 lexical items "come to mind" first. Grammatical transpositions seem to be considered only when the grammatical feature in the L_1 text has no counterpart in the L_2, and lexical mechanisms have failed. Even though it violates Occam's Razor, translators should attempt to encode grammatically what has been expressed lexically. The translator into English could use expanded forms and present perfect constructions where the German original had used lexical means such as explicit objects (as in the examples given) or adverbs. There are also non-finite constructions such as gerunds, participles, and infinitives which serve as typically English equivalents for a variety of complex German sentence structures.

At this point, we are abandoning the subject of cohesion. The correct grammatical translation of a sentence like *er macht das nun schon seit mehr als zwanzig Jahren* by "he has been doing this for more than twenty years" is not really a textual problem. It can be solved perfectly at the sentence level. There is structure but not texture. It would be a misuse of the term cohesion to say that grammar makes sentences cohesive. There are enough truly textual relations that provide grammatical cohesion. Examples of such relations include reference, substitution, ellipsis, and conjunction (Halliday and Hasan 1976). All of them can be used effectively in translation.

Intertextuality

Linguistic markers of grammatical and lexical cohesion are distributed throughout L_1 and L_2 texts. Any individual sentence or collocation in the L_2 text may or may not contain a cohesion marker. Cohesion is experienced when individual sentences are processed successively as connected segments of the text. The reader of a target text cannot determine whether isolated structures or collocations are inappropriate, strange, awkward, or incorrect. These determinations can only be made with reference to cohesion. It is only in the larger linguistic context that a phrase or collocation is judged to be out of place. Newmark (1981), Duff (1981), and Nida and Taber (1969) have analyzed lexical and grammatical discrepancies in translations identified by L_2 readers as impaired. The cause of the impairment is not always apparent to the L_2 reader. The typical reader does not always recognize the grammatical or lexical fault that is to blame. Even so, the L_2 reader's expectation of a "normal" use of language in the text is violated. The textual discontinuities clash with the reader's experience of the use of language in other texts. The L_2 user rarely takes issue with any single aspect of the translation. He or she reacts to their cumulative effect. The flawed textual profile distances the translated L_2 text from natural L_2 texts. Duff (1981, xi) comments on this distancing when he writes, "I had been wondering why it is that translation, no matter how competent, often reads like a 'foreign' tongue. I wanted to find out what we mean when we say, instinctively, 'it sounds wrong'. And why we find it sometimes difficult to explain this feeling."

The impression that a translation "sounds wrong" comes from violations of a reader's textual expectations. The reader has in mind a set of tacit expectations about what the text "should be like." This set of expectations is a product of *intertextuality*. The concept refers to "the relationship between a given text and other relevant texts encountered in prior experience." It is proposed as the seventh and final determinant of textuality (Beaugrande and Dressler 1981, 10, 182–208; Beaugrande 1980a, 20).

Intertextuality may be the most important aspect of textuality for the translator. It is not the result of the presence or absence of any single grammatical or lexical pattern in a text. It is a function of a configuration of grammatical and lexical properties. Intertextuality is a global pattern which the reader compares to pre-existing cognitive templates abstracted from experience. Intertextuality is a property of "being like other texts of this kind" which readers attribute to texts.

By using parallel texts as guides, a translator is consciously reconfiguring elements of intentionality, acceptability, situationality informativity, coherence, and cohesion to conform to the textual expectations of the L_2 target audience. One might also speak of textual conventions. It may be useful to distinguish between textual expectations and textual conventions. Textual conventions are usually more explicit; there may be rules and guidelines for creating the text, as for instance international patent structure. Usually the translator's understanding of the textuality of the target text is less explicit. It is a less formal recognition of the requirements of the L_2 "communicative culture." Beaugrande and Dressler (1981, 206) suggest that "The whole notion of textuality may depend upon exploring the influence of intertextuality as a procedural control upon communicative activities at large."

The patterns of expectation that a reader applies to the translation are also applied to natural texts in the target language. The reader recognizes most of these texts as natural and not as translations. If the translator wants to create a translation that appears natural, then he or she should create a text whose linguistic surface evokes a similar recognition. The translation has to possess the intertextuality of the target culture's natural texts. The constraints that intertextuality places on the translator are decisive and direct. They have discrete effects on the tangible surface expression of the translation. The target text enters into a relationship with original L_2 texts; the translation has to compete with those indigenous representations. Only in special cases, where the translator or client requires the preservation of source text elements, as in Venuti's resistive translation, can translators ignore the intertextuality of the target (Neubert 1980). Every translation can be seen as having a double intertextuality. The source text has intertextual relationships with other source-language texts. The translation will establish new relationships with existing L_2 texts. The translator cannot ignore the relationship between target text and original text. Confronted with this double intertextuality, the translator must act in favor of the target language text world. Even in resistive translation the translator is not free to ignore intertextuality; source-centered translation simply uses source-text intertextuality as its procedural control.

The L_2 community demands translation because it has a need for it. The L_2 community needs access to the information in L_1 texts. Translators meet this demand by mediating source text and target text intertextuality. A translation might be said to have *mediated intertextuality*. This characterization is in accordance with our definition of translation as text-induced text production (Neubert 1980). Using this definition, an L_1 text is not translated into the target language. It is translated into an L_2 text approached by L_2 users as if it were a naturally occurring instance of their communicative culture. L_2 users may ascribe certain irregular features of a translation (irregular in the sense that they run counter to L_2 intertextuality standards) to interference from the L_1. This is not very common. L_2 readers are usually in no position to recognize a text as a translation. They tend to perceive the translation as an L_2 text which meets (or does not meet) specific communicative needs and interests. Only in extreme cases (for example, early instruction manuals for Japanese electronics in the fifties and sixties) are translations recognized as such.

In literary translation, resistance to target text intertextuality cannot be justified by recourse to the reader. The argument for resistive, non-fluent translation replaces the communicative needs of the target reader with the communicative needs of the critic or special reader. This is certainly legitimate, because each translation is as a response to a particular translation situation. We should not, however, assume that all readers have needs which match those of the critic. Resistive translation may meet the needs of special groups or "hypothetical" readers created as didactic foils by the translator interested in the preservation of cultural difference. It may even be translation for the translator's sake.

Intertextuality provides a method for unifying method and goal in translation. A text is embedded in the communicative context that provides the textual resources of a language.[58] The communicative context cannot be separated from the communicative goals of the community. If you want to achieve something by communicating, there are only a limited number of ways to do it. A speaker or writer is always constrained by expected forms of speaking or writing. A translator must match these expected forms to the target text in order to achieve his or her objectives. The translator must create the right text to match the right goal. Deviations from the expected forms may occur over a broad range. Deviations may occur at all levels, from the overall organization of the text, down to individual words and constructions. Deviations can occur in monolingual communication as well as in bilingually mediated communication. In source texts, deviations may be attributed to intertextual incompetence (the writer doesn't know how to write). In translations they are usually the result of an objective divergence between the textual conventions of the two communicative communities and the translator's failure to mediate the divergence. Mediated intertextuality puts the L_1 text at the disposal of the L_2 communicative community by embedding it in the communicative matrix of the L_2. The translator extends the communicative reach of the L_1 text. Interestingly enough, it might also be possible to create exotic intertextual hybrids. By allowing the intertextuality of the L_1 text to "show through" in the L_2 text, the translator can make it possible for L_2 readers to acquaint themselves with the communicative culture of the L_1. The range of possibilities in translation extends from the perfectly fluent target text, which may become a "better" text than the source, to the truly incompetent translation, which has abandoned both target and source intertextuality. The incompetent translation may be no more than a blurred non-text.

Intertextuality is a significant factor in determining the linguistic forms that different kinds of texts can assume. Intertextuality is related to the notion of text type. Intertextual distinctions are first-order text-typological distinctions. They are regions of expectation and recognition with fuzzy edges. Within the region most users will identify a text as belonging to a certain category. They may even give this category a name. Outside the region of recognition, the user will identify the text as belonging to some other type, or perhaps to no type. At the fuzzy edge, the text user may recognize some hybrid. Intertextuality is based on what the text user, not the text analyst, expects to see in the text. Scientific texts and modern poems have different intertextuality. Scientific texts have more constraints on their textual appearance than modern poems. Intertextuality allows readers to identify scientific texts and poems as different types of texts. Their experience with previous instances of these two kinds of texts has taught them to look for different linguistic markers. They expect to see those markers in different degrees of concentration and in different configurations. Translators must be aware of the inherent fuzziness of intertextuality. No particular marker cues the reader, identifying the text as belonging to a certain category. The appearance of specific markers can only be probabilistically described. The markers have a certain probability of appearing in specific kinds of texts. The translator must grapple with the fact that it is a configuration of markers, not any single marker, which allows the reader to give a textual identity to the text. The configurations are fluid and the boundaries which separate one complex of configurations from another are fuzzy.

Some examples, particularly in written communication, stand out as almost ideal models of certain discourse types. These texts possess most of the markers that are usual in the configuration. Others may have fewer features and yet still be identifiable. The inherent fuzziness of intertextual distinctions reflects the dynamics of linguistic interaction; it is an expression of the dialectics of language use and intertextuality. The fluid boundaries between textual types are a reflection of the ability of the text producer to tailor the text to specific communicative goals and circumstances. There is no magic number of markers that a writer or translator "has to use." Still, if a translator does not use the right markers in the right configuration, the reader may not recognize the text as natural or normal.

Translations can influence intertextual distinctions made in the target culture. There are many translations where L_1 textuality is allowed to appear in the target text. Over a period of time, large numbers of such translations may cause L_1 textual habits to appear in L_2 texts. Language contact is primarily textual contact. It is the impact of L_1 texts on L_2 texts that produces language change. Modern communication has introduced new textual conventions into target languages. A comprehensive history detailing how information transfer is linked to the dissemination of new discourse patterns has yet to be written. As an example, consider how the translation of Latin texts into Old English led to the appearance of a variety of new grammatical and lexical structures, including participle constructions and loan formations. New structures created new ways to indicate cohesion and coherence, to enhance informativity, and to reflect situationality in texts. As a result, new discourse modes developed. Saying that the English language was enriched in the course of these translation activities is only part of the truth. Translation also introduced new knowledge and new ways of organizing knowledge. This transfer of knowledge was initiated and reinforced by the "new" Old English texts. Individual translations might have been perceived as deviant, but the cumulative effect of this kind of massive translation brought about a reconfiguration of the textual resources of the L_2. Translation can be an instrument in social and ideological change. Translations can be, and have been, used to reach social and ideological goals. A side effect of this usage may be new ways of speaking and writing. Intertextuality, for better and for worse, is a chief mediating factor in the evolution of the semantics and pragmatics of languages. It is through the incorporation of new texts, many of them translations, that languages expand their inventory of cognitive repertoires. The users of a language are offered new tools for thinking about, interpreting, and expressing the world around them.

Translation is producing an increasing internationalization of languages and texts. The twentieth century has sometimes been called (in the translation literature) "the century of translation." Of the texts read by an average reader, a significant portion are translations. In some subject areas, most of the L_2 texts are translated texts. In some societies, the primary discursive influence may be translated texts. Consider the translation of technological texts into the languages of Third World countries (Harris 1983). The situation is not entirely different in countries whose languages are more widely spoken. Many Spanish medical texts exhibit an "English-like" quality because of the influence of translations and the fact that Spanish doctors read English medical texts (Talentino 1991). Intertextual features such as formatting and terminological structure tend to become international. These "international" intertextual features occur regularly in subject-area texts written in a variety of structurally different languages like English, Russian, or Japanese.

This internationalization can exist in political and journalistic texts as well. But there are forces which also support intertextual separation. Because of the profound ideological split between the democratic West and the Communist East, many texts of the same "supposed" type were quite distinct textually. Journalistic texts in Russian were not the same as those in American English newspapers. Some of the difference was quite naturally the result of textual tradition, but some of it was deliberate and ideologically motivated. The communicative aims were different, and so were the textual mechanisms used to achieve those aims. Intertextual separation can also occur in groups where linguistic and textual traditions were once shared. Consider the differences in journalistic discourse between the former German Democratic Republic and the Federal Republic of Germany. A comparison of *Pravda* and *Neues Deutschland,* organs of the ruling parties of two communist countries, yields striking intertextual similarities. These two papers were more like one another than *Neues Deutschland* was like the *Frankfurter Allgemeine Zeitung.* Intertextual similarity existed in spite of linguistic and cultural difference. It was a result of the massive translation of Soviet political and journalistic texts in East Germany and of the deliberate use of Soviet discourse by East German politicians. In East Germany it was the rule to immediately publish translations of all Soviet Communist party pronouncements; newspapers in the one-time German Democratic Republic acted as mouthpieces for political views originally expressed in Russian texts. There was, in fact, a weekly magazine called *Die Presse der Sowjetunion* that regularly published articles about Soviet life (with an emphasis on the official word).

The political events of 1989, including the fall of the Berlin wall and the democratization of the socialist countries of the old Eastern bloc, very quickly changed the political discourse of the East. Almost overnight journalists of the old order have unlearned old discursive habits and taken their textual cues from their Western colleagues. The transition was effected by critically-minded journalists already oriented toward the West. Intertextual alignment replaced intertextual separation.

The systems of the English, Russian, and German languages are neutral with regard to the political content they are used to propagate. Yet textual arrangement, as a consistent pattern of textual markers, can be used to signal shared political values. Very little has appeared in the literature about methods for describing how mutual political knowledge constrains grammatical and lexical choices to produce certain political text types. The translator of political texts is acutely aware of the cues and symbolic conventions that appear in texts. Experience with parallel texts has helped the translator identify the textual features whose appearance in certain configurations cues the reader that a certain textual strategy is being used. These features may include collocations, metaphors, key words, terminological traditions, historical allusions, structural progressions, and conventions for introducing names and persons. They may include references to status and social role. This inventory is by no means exhaustive. The patterned occurrence of these and a myriad other features comprises the textual regions of expectation that we call intertextuality.

Patterned expectations of the text lead the reader to categorize texts. This categorization is not explicit. The reader does not always label the category of the text, but he or she is able to tell one kind of text from another. Readers can distinguish newspaper articles from scientific papers and propaganda pieces from reporting. Readers form a first-order typology of texts based on differences in textual expectation. It should be possible to study this naive text typology by empirical means. The text typologies of the translator or text typologist should be second-order text typologies based on observations of the expectations and identifications of the text user. Second-order empirical typologies will be more useful to translators than abstract text typologies that are based more on reflection than on observation. Translators are extremely sensitive to text-typological issues because their jobs rely on an awareness of the cues and expectations typical of L_2 texts. Their awareness is not the first-order awareness of the reader, because this awareness is largely reactive. It is visible only when expectations are violated. The translator must have an explicit and not a tacit understanding of the intertextuality of the source and target language texts. The translator recognizes the fact that translation is an exercise in cross-cultural and cross-linguistic intertextuality. Translation is mediated intertextuality.

FOUR

Translation as Result

Translation Evolution

The title of this volume, *Translation as Text*, emphasizes the fact that translations are texts and that the processes of translation are primarily textual processes. The target text is produced as the result of a careful matching process that considers the complex relationships between the text world of the L_1 text and the text world of the L_2 text. A finished translation, the translation finally released into the hands of the client or reader, is a final translation result. One might be tempted to say that at this point the translation process is complete. But, is the process really complete? The decisions made by the translator during the creative phase of the translation may have open-ended effects on L_2 readers. As long as the translation is read, the linguistic cues the translator has chosen will have an effect. Certainly, the creative phase comes to an end when the translator gives the text to a reader. A new phase of the translation process begins when the reader uses the translator's cues and markers in active text comprehension. During the stage of active translation, the translator is the active partner and the reader is only a projected partner. In the second stage of translation, the reader takes center stage. Linguistic expressions at the textual surface are the only remnants of the translator's presence. Ironically, the more effective a translation is, the more difficult it is to detect the presence of the translator. The best pragmatic translations are never recognized as translations because they are accepted as native texts. The translation merges imperceptibly with the world of L_2 texts. The translator and his or her understanding of textuality are the agents of that merger.

Some translations do not rest comfortably in the target text world. It may be the case that certain literary translations will need to be re-translated because linguistic usages, textual conventions, and sociocultural understandings have changed. The translation situations that existed when they were first produced have altered, and the translations are now found wanting. In these cases, a kind of translation morphogenesis occurs. The translation goes through cycles of active translation and critical reading. Most non-literary translations do not participate in this cycle. Pragmatic texts are rarely retranslated. The translation situations that evoked their original transfer were unique. Practical translations are more tightly bound to the pragmatic conditions of their creation than literary translations. Usually, the need for the translation has disappeared. Once they are translated, pragmatic texts become an integral part of the textual system of the target culture. If they are well translated, they will not be recognized as translations. An effective practical translation will conform to the textuality standards of the target culture, and their evolution as translations will be over.

Certain literary translations may be so favorably received that they become part of the target culture's textual canon. Attempts by well-intentioned modern translators to create more contemporary versions may meet with resistance. Schlegel and Tieck's translations of Shakespeare in the nineteenth century and Luther's sixteenth-century translation of the Bible still enjoy a greater popularity in some countries than more recent translations.

Even if we accept the notion of translation morphogenesis, this does not imply that "descendants" of the original translation are more advanced. Consider Bible translation. The *Simple English New Testament,* the *New International Revised Standard,* and the *Living Bible* are certainly quite different from the *King James Version.* These different translations have an equal right to exist. Each version is the result of a particular translation situation. Different purposes and different needs are expressed in the translation; given the different situations, each may be perfectly adapted to its purpose.

Text Types

A translation's ability to merge with native texts comes from its capacity to adopt the textual features of the native text. Every translation is characterized by a particular configuration of textual features. Situation, intent, informativity, and the other determinants of textuality are accounted for and manipulated by the translator. The configuration of textual features in the text is controlled to match the configurations expected by L_2 text readers. The L_2 user has a set of textual expectations which control his or her reaction to the text. Such expectations are not necessarily conscious. Like most everyday knowledge, textual knowledge can be verified only in violation. Although users cannot specify what is wrong with a text in precise terms, they can usually relate their general impressions. They can tell when the text goes astray. Violations of textual structure may have physical consequences. Readers may have to re-read a text several times. They may throw a badly translated instruction manual down in disgust.

Readers don't look for the same configurations of markers in every text they read. They can recognize particular configurations of textual characteristics as a particular "type" of text. This first-order text typology is naive. It is constructed, not so much as a result of analytic reflection, but as an accretion of experience. For instance, as the result of experience with "personal letters" a particular broad pattern of textual features is associated with a specific label. The translator's recognition of the first-order typology of his or her readers is a significant part of translation expertise. The professional scholar's text typologies are useful ways to represent the general nature of texts. They are useful to the practicing translator only if they help to make translation decisions that produce target texts which match target reader expectations. Both the translator and the professional text scholar must have a second-order understanding of the social distribution of textual knowledge. This second-order understanding is a description of the first-order understandings of translation users. The translator's second-order knowledge is built from experience, from the collection of parallel texts, and from consultation with target language readers and experts. The translator's second-order text typologies are rarely as explicit and formal as those of the scholarly text analyst, but they do not need to be. The translator is a practical text analyst. He or she first needs to determine what type of text must be created. The translator will then need to consciously manipulate and combine those textual features necessary to make the text an instance of the text type in the target language community.

In his discussion of discourse strategies, Gumperz (1982, 1) makes the crucial point that "communication is a social activity requiring the coordinated efforts of two or more individuals. Mere talk to produce sentences, no matter how well formed or elegant the outcome, does not by itself constitute communication." The translator is a partner in a communicative activity. The translator's L_2 textual competence works against the background of a communicative partnership. The conditions under which a text is said to be "acceptable" or "appropriate" are not determined by the translator. The translator is the minor partner in the communicative interaction. The conditions of acceptability are determined by the text reader and only reflected by the translator. It is the translator who must coordinate text production to match the textual knowledge of the target reader.

A translator's first-order text types reflect socially typified communicative procedures. Such procedures are socially distributed discursive mechanisms intended for use in certain kinds of situations. Text types are almost as heterogeneous as the social situations in which they are used. They are incorporated in the text user's knowledge of social activity. As such, the translator's use of a text type requires the activation of particular cognitive frames and the invocation of specific interactional scenarios. Text type understandings are inputs to the translator's procedural knowledge-base. The translator uses a knowledge of text types to assemble the linguistic material available in the system of a target language and create socially efficient, situationally effective, and communicatively appropriate configurations.[59]

Texts are instances of the activation of socially distributed communicative procedures. Their textual surfaces carry linguistic markers which result from the application of underlying procedural understandings. The communicative procedures of the L_2 are not evenly distributed. Not all readers have equal access to the total textual potential of their culture. Their experience with texts is never identical, and their personal communicative histories may be quite diverse. Textual experience is built up through early socialization, public education, and special training. Some first-order textual types are broadly distributed. An example is the *personal letter* text type. Other textual types, such as repair manuals, may be more narrowly distributed. The total textual knowledge of a culture is never coincident with the textual knowledge of a single individual. Text types are labels for complexes of receptive expectations and productive procedures. Text types act to define sets of socially situated textual instances which share certain features.

Individual texts can only be understood when they make sense in the context of a reader's social relations. They have to cohere with the reader's relationship to the text producer and understanding of the purpose of what is being communicated. The text user identifies specific situations with specific communicative procedures. A reader is motivated to act and react in those situations as a result of a "motivational framework generated from stored knowledge" (Garnham 1983, 152). Thus, text types are socially institutionalized tools whose application has been learned as a form of specific social knowledge (Stein 1982, 330).

A knowledge of text types is not acquired in addition to words and grammar but in conjunction with them. The linguistic copresence of forms and structures in particular texts attaches to mentally stored frames. As experience with texts accrues, the distributions of linguistic forms in the texts lose their immediate contexts. They are associated in a more abstract way with types of texts and less with specific instances. The use of linguistic elements in specific kinds of texts is an interplay of text and text type. Characteristic distributions of linguistic markers trigger textual knowledge frames. Recognition of the triggering effect, however, leads authors and writers to produce those distributions in texts. Text types are a combination of receptive expectation and productive procedure.

Text types operate as procedural knowledge because configurations of textual markers (patterns of linguistic material) are associated with abstract frames. The specific configuration of textual markers in a text type cannot, however, be identified with a simple checklist of textual markers. A reader's ability to recognize a particular distribution of features as a specific type of text does not result from scanning the text for required elements. Producing a text so that it will be recognized as an instance of a particular text type is not a simple matter of introducing, element by element, all of the features required to mark it as a member of that type. A checklist analysis of texts might be a useful analytic tool, but it probably does not represent the actual ways readers and writers use text types.

The translation scholar's view of text types has to take into account a more realistic view of the sophisticated contextualization of textual markers that occurs in social activity. While it is true that some textual types like patents and certain types of poetry are governed by formal rules, most other text types cannot be described as neatly. Even in patents the formal requirements do not necessarily extend to all levels of the text. With patents the formal requirements apply at more general levels of the text. They do not deal with the more concrete levels of grammatical and lexical cohesion. There may be prescribed global formats but no prescriptions for the internal structure of paragraphs or sections. Most texts are not produced from pre-existent formal prescriptions. The translator's task would be simpler if this were the case. The formal prescriptions would describe textual templates. Such templates would have characteristic groups of invariant structures interspersed with variant structures. The variant structures would be filled in when a communicative context was provided. The following document is an example of a textual template.

Assignment of Lease

_____ and _____ , Lessees of that certain lease dated _____ , by and between _____ Lessor and _____ Lessee, and pertaining to that certain _____ do hereby assign their right, title and interest in and to said lease to _____ , whose address shall henceforth be _____ . It is agreed and understood that this assignment is contingent upon satisfactory compliance with the terms and provisions of the lease.

Witnesses:

_____

_____

Acceptance

We, _____ , hereby accept the above assignment and subject ourselves to all the promises and covenants therein contained. We fully understand that this assignment is contingent upon the making of timely payments on the lease and complying with all the terms and provisions of the lease.

Witnesses:

_____

_____

Consent

_____ , landlord and lessor under the above lease hereby consents to the assignment of said lease from _____ to _____ .

By: _____
Attest: _____

The number of texts which can be described in this way is limited. While it is true that texts represent concretely organized social knowledge, the knowledge is usually not organized in a formulaic way. The translator must understand the linguistic consistency of a text type as an organized collection of social understandings about texts rather than as a fixed template. If a text belongs to a particular text type, then its "discourse level conventions reflect prolonged interactive experience by individuals cooperating in institutionalized settings in the pursuit of (more or less) shared goals" (Gumperz 1982, 209).

Discourse conventions are a communicative practice that operates within the framework of similar, but not identical, social contexts. Every instance of communication within a particular communicative context produces a textual instance. Because each social context is different, the actual texts associated with them are different. A textual type is a typification of the variant instances that cluster around a generalized social context. The textual type *business contract* cannot be separated from the social context of contract negotiation. The conventional features of business contracts as a class of textual instances is a result of accrued experience of contract negotiation. The linguistic surface of the contract reflects the scenarios (abstract texts) attached to the social setting. The first-order textual type is not a formula or a template but an abstraction derived from experience. It is an abstraction derived from texts experienced in specific social circumstances. The text type is not a textual pattern but an organized set of expectations and recognitions that can be used to generate patterns. Such sets of expectations and recognitions are not at all like the clear-cut text types of the text analyst. The first-order text type is actually a *prototype*.

Prototypes

The prototype is not a text even though it has accrued from the experience of texts. A prototype is a socially conditioned mode of organizing knowledge in spoken or written discourse. We use the word *prototype* to distinguish the first-order types we have just discussed from the analytic text types of text typologists. Specific configurations of textual markers in any particular text do not have an all-or-nothing relationship to the prototype. The features of any single textual instance never exhaust the features available in the prototype. An exhaustive listing of the features present in a large collection of textual instances "of the same type" do not define the prototype. The prototype is not just a frame full of characteristic textual features. It is also a set of situation-specific ways to organize the features. Contexts interact with prototypes to produce textual instances. Prototypes are knowledge structures applied in the production and interpretation of texts. As such, they are more than the sum of many instances of texts. Similarly, an instance is not determined by the prototype alone. A textual instance is always conditioned by the social situation. Each individual textual instance uses some, but not all, of the possibilities offered by the prototype. The selection of markers is conditioned by pragmatic variables interacting with the prototype at the time of text production.

The interdependence of prototype and physical text is a product of the variability of the social circumstances in which textual instances emerge. There is a constant interplay between the stability provided by the shared expectation structure of the prototype and the variability of textual circumstances. This interplay imparts a characteristic historicity to texts. They evolve dynamically through time. There is never a perfect balance between prototype and social situation; the textual instance is a compromise where the stability of textual understandings plays off against the unique demands of the communicative situation. Only in unusual circumstances, where the communicative situation itself is prescribed, do textual instances become more static and tend to converge. Legal texts are a good example of cases where the communicative situations are prescribed. The extreme stability of the situation produces conformity in the textual instances.

Thus, the features associated with a prototype are always in a state of flux. Today's mandatory feature may be optional tomorrow. Features associated with one kind of text may appear in other kinds of texts. New clusters of textual instances appear as new prototypes evolving under dynamic social circumstances. The following newspaper article presents a fascinating glimpse of textual evolution in progress. A quarterly report and a comic book are merged into a new hybrid text sharing features of both the parent prototypes (*Record Courier*, 18 December 1991):

Marvel gets comical with quarterly report

Now public Marvel Entertainment Group Inc. has published its first quarterly report to shareholders as a four-page color comic book starring The Incredible Hulk and The Amazing Spider-Man.

"Things have sure changed around here!" says the Hulk, bursting from a business suit.

Any given feature or cluster of features may be associated with more than one type of text. The boundaries between prototypes are not rigid. We might think of prototypes as "fuzzy types" whose edges shade off into other prototypes. Textual instances may have "degrees of belonging" to the prototype. Lakoff's classic example of the bird prototype comes to mind. The robin is considered more of a bird than a penguin. Yet, they are both still recognized as birds. Consider business letters as an example. There are textual instances of business letters clearly recognizable as belonging to the type. The appearance and characteristic organization of certain textual markers allows a reader to immediately recognize the type. There may be other instances that exhibit fewer features but are still recognizable as business letters. When does a business letter cease to be recognizable as such? There is no single feature which elicits recognition and acceptance. There is a complex impression on the reader which is cued by associations of linguistic elements at the textual surface. Substitution, deletion, reconfiguration, and addition of markers can imperceptibly move a textual instance away from the potential for distinct recognition. These changes can lead the reader to classify the text as another type, as some flawed form of a recognizable type, or as some hybrid type. Hybrids, though novel, may still be communicatively acceptable because they match the demands of the situation. Their overall character induces a general recognition of "textness." This implies that a text may be recognized as a text even if it cannot be associated with a particular text type. Texts can exhibit textuality without exhibiting prototypicality.

Prototypes organize our understanding of textuality. They define particular regions of textuality as serving particular communicative functions. Prototypicality occurs within the broader framework of textuality. Prototypes function in the context of social goals; therefore, they cannot be considered prescriptions. They are a discursive means to reach specific ends, and they are subordinated to those ends. Prototypes are what Marx called *soziale Verkehrsformen*.[60] They are particular ways of speaking and writing accepted at a particular time in history by particular communicating subgroups.

Prototypes both determine social process and are determined by social process; this dual character makes them difficult to describe. Part of the difficulty is due to their complete integration of social function, information content, and textual form. A major research problem in text linguistics is differentiating textual content, textual form, and textual function.

For instance, one of the most common text classification systems separates texts into descriptive, narrative, and argumentative categories. This division fails to capture the social function of form and content. Other approaches, based on the traditions of classical rhetoric, have developed elaborate descriptive systems under names like functional stylistics, discourse analysis, and ethnomethodology. Some of these systems have produced impressive descriptions that detail correspondences between suprasentential arrangements and patterns of social interaction. The conceptual instruments these approaches provide are not precise enough to yield a fully satisfactory descriptive and explanatory model of the prototype. Nevertheless, concepts derived from these approaches are universally applied in translation studies. Some of the concepts that appear in the literature of discourse analysis and functional stylistics include descriptives like *everyday, scientific, journalistic, official,* and *literary.* There are also labels for textual categories: *greetings, conversations, letters, news stories, headlines, political speeches, patents, public notices, injunctions, novels,* and *poems.*

All of these terms refer to important interactional properties of texts. Most of these concepts, however, emphasize specific aspects of textuality at the expense of others. The concepts are too coarse. They evoke, but do not specify, the full range of features available in prototypes.[61] Texts are used to realize social goals. As such, they display intentionality. The text's ability to achieve an author's or translator's intent is constrained by the acceptability conditions active in the situation. Acceptability conditions may place constraints on information structure, coherence patterns, and lexical/grammatical cohesion. Traditional text type descriptives do not account for this complexity because of their focus on the results of textual processes. Prototypes, on the other hand, emphasize the synthesis of textual knowledge and textual process. Prototypes account for all of the features of textuality: intentionality, acceptability, situationality, informativity, coherence, cohesion, and intertextuality. Identifying the linguistic mechanisms that can be used to integrate these seven textual features in target texts is the translator's main task. It is a task that the translator must carry out within the scope of target culture prototypes.

While it is true that each text is a singular event in a unique social situation, it is also true that textual instances reflect underlying social norms. In spite of the uniqueness of each communicative act, social norms allow the prototype to function as a model for mediating between past experience and future goals. The prototype yields a superstructure that outlines for us the ways we can communicate. Like the old journalistic rule, this superstructure details the who, what, when, where, and how of textual communication (Van Dijk 1980, 107).

Prototypical superstructures reflect both the uniformity and diversity of social discourse. The empirical study of textual instances reveals no clear-cut criterial system of texts. As we have said, prototypes are not checklists. It is always possible to isolate some features that belong to a so-called text type. For instance, "text books" always have pedagogical intent. This intent is reflected in a typical presentation and organization of information content. At specific grade levels there may be characteristic syntax and lexical usages. A number of typical "instructional" scenarios can be expected. Are these shared features enough to describe a "prototype text book"? Could an abstract of all the common features of text books used in schools provide the basis for identifying a textual superstructure? Would this superstructure be a useful model for authors and translators? The effort might be useful to some degree. The empirical analysis of these texts would have to be fine-grained enough to allow a translator to predict the actual linguistic mechanisms used to create textuality.

Most text typology is reductive. It reduces the diversity of actual texts by creating a small number of (often) mutually exclusive categories. Text typology relies on the identification of discriminant features. This analytic approach may produce an enlightening view of the texts available in a culture but provides little guidance for the translator. Reduction whittles away the detail the translator requires. Prototype analysis is particularizing and provides a more detailed analysis of actual textual instances. Prototypes capture more detail because they account for all the determinants of textuality. Prototypes reflect patterns of actual communicative events. Text typologies are abstractions based on the relics of communicative events.

As a practical matter, translators engage in prototype analysis by collecting and studying examples of the texts that their readers and clients actually use. This first-order analysis makes them aware of the actual linguistic mechanisms that are used to achieve textuality. Practicing translators use prototype analysis when they collect parallel texts and apply the textual profiles of those texts as guides for inducing textuality in their translations. The empirical second-order analysis of prototypes can only be based on the collection and analysis of these same socially-situated texts. It is not our task here to specify how this should be done. We are concerned primarily with how prototypes can be used by the translator.

Translators have to focus on the linguistic particulars of the L_2 prototype. Abstract criterial features are of little use. Identification of the abstract text type of the translation is only a starting point. This preliminary identification must be followed by the study of similarly situated texts. These parallel texts give the translator discrete points of reference which can be factored into the mental model of the text. These discrete points of reference, abstracted from L_2 textual instances, are a manifestation of the L_2 prototype. Using these instances as a guide, the translator *re-textures* the source text. The end result is a text with an L_2 superstructure (Neubert 1984; Snell-Hornby 1988; Bühler 1988).

The translator guides the development of the target text by monitoring its conformance to the prototype. The prototype that a translator uses is entirely dependent on the textual instances he or she is aware of. This implies that better translation would be a result of a greater awareness of the range of textual instances in the target culture. On the other hand, one or two good parallel texts, carefully selected, might also suffice. Prototypes are not quantitative entities; they are qualitative entities.

When a translator uses a prototype, he or she is using it as a mechanism for evaluating the "textness" of the target text. The prototype should lead the translator to ask critical questions. Does the translation consider that L_2 readers might not have the required mutual knowledge? How can gaps in mutual knowledge be rectified by the introduction of new material? How will this new material affect the informativity of the text? Do these changes require alterations in the coherence patterns of the text? Does the situationality of the L_2 text require the translator to re-interpret the intentionality of the original? Do lexical attachments to specific L_2 frames make it necessary to modify the lexical surface of the L_2 text? Prototypical analysis is a way of systematically accounting for the textuality of a translation using a thorough understanding of target culture parallel texts as a guide.

We have said that prototypes are not templates. The translator must systematically account for the factors which determine the textuality of the translation. Because prototypes do not specify the contents of specific textual instances, there are situations where the translator has to make choices that are beyond the scope of the prototype. For instance, when does situational context override an author's intent? When should L_2 conventions be disregarded and L_1 textuality preserved? Questions of this type transcend prototypicality. Prototypes only lead the translator to the textual surface. They do not dictate broader strategic decisions. A prototype is only a useful guide when the situationality and intentionality of the text has been determined. Situational factors cause the translator to abandon one prototype for another.

Textual Meaning

The translator's use of prototypes is not independent of the meanings in the text. Textuality is not an end in itself. Language has been developed as a mechanism for the exchange of meaning.[62] Therefore, important semantic questions for the translator relate to what happens to linguistic carriers of meaning (words, sentences, morphemes) when they are combined in texts. How are local units of meaning synthesized into more global units of *textual meaning*? The concept of prototype deals with patterns of the linguistic surface that are accepted and expected in the target culture. Textual meaning, on the other hand, refers to semantic patterns that are carried in the text and experienced as a connected whole. Textual meaning and prototype are combined by the translator to communicate meaning in recognizable textual packages.

Textual meaning is formed in the translator's mind only after he or she has understood the L_1 text. An understanding of the text may come from a close reading of the full text, or it may derive from skimming, reading in sections, or other comprehension strategies. L_1 textual meaning is a kind of mental model that functions as the determinant of the textual meaning of the L_2.[63] The translator evaluates L_2 linguistic resources and uses them in the target text if they are consistent with the textual meaning of the L_1. The prototype interacts with textual meaning to condition the precise linguistic expressions that are used. The translator can only use textual meaning as a guide if it can accommodate all of the important linkages between meaning and the textuality conferred by prototypes.[64] Textual meaning and textual prototypes are linked. Textual meaning provides the global semantic structure that is given linguistic expression through the application of a prototype.

Textual meaning is more than the accumulation or aggregation of smaller meaning units. Textual meanings are independent global units of cognition and communication that reflect relationships with past, present, and future textual meanings. They are discrete communicative units with semantic and pragmatic relationships to other texts (Van Dijk 1980, 90). For example, there is an entailment relation that links a summary with the text it summarizes. Consider the pragmatic linkages between the legal texts generated by the interactions of judge, prosecutor, defense attorney, defendant, and witnesses at a trial. Each of these legal roles is associated with an ensemble of texts. The textual meanings of the texts are related because of the social norms that govern the activities of the participants.

The textual meanings of discrete texts are connected by semantic links and pragmatic links. The translator of a computer manual may consult a textbook on computers to resolve a terminological question. The link between the two texts is a semantic one. The link between the translation of a legal brief and a parallel legal brief in the target language is a pragmatic link. Parallel text and translation need not be on the same subject. They are, however, addressed to the same kind of audience, and they reflect the same intentionality. Translators consult background texts because these texts have semantic connections to the prospective target text. They consult parallel texts because of the prototypic and pragmatic relationships that target text and parallel text share.

Macrostructures and Macrorules

The link between L_1 textual meaning and L_2 textual meaning is semantic. The semantic ties are overlaid by pragmatic and contextual constraints related to situation and the target language prototype. The meanings of the L_1 text (to be translated) and the meaning of the (translated) L_2 text have a specific semantic relationship. The global semantic structures of the two texts conform predictably to one another but are not identical. The semantic structures are not identical because of the modifications required when textual meanings are merged with prototypical superstructures. When textual meaning and prototype come together, the result is *textualized meaning*. The global semantic meaning (or global proposition) textualized by the prototype yields a textual superstructure. The textual superstructure is a textualized global proposition.

Textual superstructures can be decomposed into an ordered set of semantic macrostructures. Macrostructures reflect typical textualized semantic patterns of L_1 and L_2. A semantic macrostructure is a textualized semantic macroproposition.

Macropropositions are intermediate semantic structures that are just underneath the main themes of the text (the global proposition). They exist at levels of "rising" generality (Neubert 1987). At lower, more particular levels, textual meaning decomposes into its ultimate constituents, atomic micropropositions. Textualized micropropositions are microstructures. For the purposes of illustration, it might be useful to imagine the propositional structure of a text as a kind of tree structure. The global proposition of the text is at the root of the tree and macropropositions are at intermediate nodes. Atomic micropropositions are the terminal branches of the semantic tree.

Macropropositions are topicalizations of lower level propositions. These higher level intermediate structures can be derived from lower level structures by so-called macro-rules. "These rules are a kind of semantic derivation or inference rule: They derive macrostructures from microstructures" (Van Dijk 1980, 46). The successive application of such rules yields the global meaning of the text.[65]

Macrorules are hypothetical representations of text comprehension procedures. They are an attempt to explain how the readers of a translation or other text can synthesize larger meaning units from the smaller meaning units encountered sequentially at the textual surface. Text comprehension presupposes a bottom-up synthesis of the global meaning. Text production presumes a top-down derivation of atomic micropropositions from more global semantic structures.

In the context of translation we cannot assume that target text macropropositions and, by extension, the global proposition they represent are the direct result of sentence by sentence meaning transfer. Target text macropropositions must be created by the translator as the result of a new top-down production. The translator has to evaluate sections of the source text for their meaning. He or she must place these meanings in the target text in such a way that the reader is led to derive the appropriate intermediate and final macrostructures. The translator is, in a sense, building a map for the target text reader to follow in the bottom-up construction of the textual meaning of the translation (Gutt 1990).

Attempts have been made to classify the macrorules that are used to construct textual meaning. Three different types of macrorules have been described: deletion rules, generalization rules, and construction rules. Each defines a characteristic way of linking lower-order with higher-order meanings.

Deletion macrorules delete irrelevant micropropositions and macropropositions. Relevance is defined against the global meaning of the text. Deletion rules are also called selection rules because they select important facts and reject unimportant ones.[66] One particular selection rule warrants some more description. If a lower-level proposition is "raised" to a higher level, perhaps even to the highest level, this is due to a zero rule. It is called a zero rule because "zero" elements were deleted. Zero rules are evident in very short texts, where "everything" is at the same semantic level. All of the meaning units are relevant.

Another macrorule, superficially similar to deletion, abstracts semantic material from lower-level propositions. The generalization rule raises certain features while ignoring others; the rule submerges specific meanings under more general meanings. Nothing is deleted, and nothing new is added. Generalization rules condense and clarify textual meaning. The closer one comes to the global proposition, the more general the macropropositions.

Construction is the third macrorule. It differs from generalization because it introduces new meaning elements into macropropositions. Construction rules are perhaps the most powerful procedures used to establish global meanings. They connect propositions represented in the text with the reader's own knowledge. The semantic material contained in the text is sequenced in such a way that it activates user knowledge in a deliberate and directed way. This activation is possible because the information trigger (in the text) and the information target (in the user's knowledge frames) are copresent. Thus, a relatively small number of textually expressed micropropositions is supplemented by a vastly larger set of textually cued, frame-derived propositions. Macropropositions are augmented by the reader's own knowledge of the world. The implication of construction is that the global meaning of the text is expanded. It contains more semantic information than was present in the actual propositions underlying the text. Expressed another way, construction allows the global meaning to be *read into* the text. Construction only works if comprehenders invest their various kinds of knowledge in the meaning construction process. Construction rules reflect the fact that textual meanings are not static constructs. The text the translator is trying to create in the L_2 is the enriched text the reader creates by the application of macrorules. This greater text is a virtual text, and the written version is only its visual incarnation.

Construction rules illustrate the interdependence of textual meaning and textuality that we spoke about earlier. When textual meaning merges with a prototype, we get textualized meaning. The sequence of linguistic markers at the textual surface has an effect on the construction of textual meaning. The sequence is the basis for the reader's bottom-up construction of the global meaning of the text. The translator is not free, however, to produce just any textual surface. The textual expectations of the target community constrain the actual linguistic mechanisms that can be applied. The influence of prototypes on textual meaning implies that the translator cannot depend solely on his or her internalized conception of the L_1 textual meaning when producing the target text. The L_1 textual meaning is a framework constraining the L_2 textual meaning. L_2 analogues of L_1 macropropositional structures are draped onto the prototypical superstructure expected in the L_2 community.

The argument for a textual approach to translation rests to a great degree on the notion of global textual meaning. It is the global meaning of a translation, re-textualized as an L_2 text, that must be matched to the original global meaning of the source text. Textual meaning is the genesis of the translator's textual strategy. The translator cannot translate words or sentences. Translators can only translate texts. When translators translate source texts, they are simultaneously creating the physical target text and the potential for the reader to generate the virtual text which it represents.

Communicative Value

The physical target text is a semantic potential. It is used by the translator as a mechanism to allow the reader to construct a complex semantic object that contains information of value to the reader. Thus, what the translator is really negotiating in the transfer of meanings from the L_1 to the L_2 text is a *communicative value*. Textual meaning is a mapping of the linguistic structures of the physical text to the reader's knowledge structures through the application of macrorules.[67] The communicative value is the pragmatic and social effect of generating this meaning. There may be multiple mappings created by different configurations of the textual determinants of situation and intent. This means that texts may have more than one communicative value, although senders normally have only a single one in mind.

One constraint on the translator's ability to create communicative value is what the user knows about the world, about language, and about the communicative event. The translator's ability to produce an L_2 text which will have communicative value is conditioned by the reader's capacity to understand linguistic cues and their references. The target text represents a potential for the L_2 reader to "read" information into the text using construction rules. Construction can only act to generate new meanings if the cues presented in the target text can trigger knowledge frames that are actually present. Take the example of a book on advanced nuclear physics. We recognize the book as a text, but its communicative value to us is limited. It is intended for specialists with a specific stock of knowledge. The linguistic surface of the text triggers knowledge frames which we do not possess. The knowledge potential of the L_2 text is never completely identical with the knowledge potential of the L_1 text.[68]

There is a *heterovalence* that arises from the different knowledge L_1 and L_2 users bring to the translation situation. Heterovalence refers to the divergence of communicative value that happens when textual meaning intersects with situational factors.

The role of translation is not just the mediation of differences in language between L_1 and L_2. Translation must also mediate the knowledge differential between L_1 and L_2. Bridging the knowledge gap calls for linguistic recoding and for the textual modifications necessary to induce appropriate textual meaning. The textual meaning has to be functionally and situationally appropriate. The text has to achieve a communicative value that reflects situational requirements as well as semantic and textual ones.

The communicative value of a translation represents a selection from the global meaning of the source text. It is not identical with textual meaning; it is an intersection of textual meaning with the resources and orientation the user brings to the text. It represents what the reader can retrieve and use from the text. This is rarely everything that is potentially retrievable from the text. Communicative value is influenced by "such factors as wants, wishes, preferences, interests, tasks, purposes, attitudes, values, and norms" (Van Dijk 1980, 201). The communicative value of the L_2 text is dependent on the *cognitive set* of the L_2 reader. This term refers to the level of *macroprocessing* at which the user functions. Macroprocessing refers to the user's ability to extract value from the text by applying macrorules. If L_2 readers succeed in extracting communicative value from a translation, it is because the translation has been adapted to their cognitive sets by a translator who is aware of "the set of factors that in a particular context of (action or) discourse processing, influences macrostructures" (Van Dijk 1980, 201).[69]

The global meaning and communicative values of the translation are created using a semantic image of the L_1 text stored in the mind of the translator. This image is modified and restructured and then re-textualized using a prototype. The retextualization should reflect the reader's cognitive set. Every single item that appears in the target text, from cohesion devices to modes of address, must be the result of a decision-making process directed toward the reader.

Sometimes a translator has a choice between two equally valid options. The textual meaning of the source text, the prototypical superstructure of the target text, and the cognitive set of the reader can all help the translator make the best choice. Once choices are made, however, the translator is progressively constrained. As the linguistic elaboration of the text increases, the translator's freedom to choose decreases. The translator must be prepared to retract original choices and modify already translated microstructures. This retraction and modification is something that the translator should not hesitate to do in the interests of the reader. If the translator is unwilling to do this, then he or she is allowing the microstructural evolution of the L_2 text to govern the translation process. Such unwillingness will always lead the translator astray.

Textual and Communicative Equivalence

The complex interaction between source text meaning and target text communicative value raises the issue of *equivalence*. Because this notion has become a major bone of contention in recent years (Snell-Hornby 1988), it deserves some discussion. Most criticisms of equivalence stem from a narrow linguistic and lexical interpretation of equivalence. It is clear that L_1 words and L_2 words are almost never equivalent in meaning. Only certain standardized terms from technical and scientific domains may be said to be equivalent. Even these terms may take on new meanings when they enter texts and become parts of discourse strategies. There is no defense for linguistic equivalence. One can make a case, however, for *textual equivalence*. Textual equivalence is not semantic equivalence between words. It is a new order of pragmatic equivalence between texts. Textual equivalence can be derived from the concept of prototype. Texts can be said to be equivalent when their textual profiles are derived from situationally and functionally equivalent prototypes. A German computer manual is situationally equivalent to an American computer manual. The intentionality of a text book in Madrid is intentionally equivalent to a text book in Cleveland. The computer manuals and text books in these two situations can be said to be equivalent because they play equivalent social and communicative roles. Their prototypes are not identical in content, but they are socially equivalent. If practicing translators did not recognize this kind of "equivalence," they would not be able to identify and choose parallel texts to guide their work. Equivalence is not identity. No text is exactly like another text. The textuality of a source text and a target text diverge at several levels. There are differences in cohesion patterns and coherence. Textual equivalence is not derived from textual identity but from the equivalent social and communicative roles played by different kinds of texts.

Textual equivalence is a useful but quite general concept. It cannot function as a practical tool for the translator and translation scholar. We have to look deeper into the translation process for another kind of equivalence. Let us imagine the following situation. A translation has been well translated. The target reader accepts it as a valid textual instance and is able to retrieve from it what he or she needs to know. The text yields a communicative value derived from the translator's proper connection of source text meaning with target culture prototype. What relationship does this new text have with the original text? We can say that the new text "stands in the place" of the original text. It is a re-textualized proxy of the source text. It conveys information to the target reader that the source text could not. Even though the textual surfaces do not match, and the semantic structure may have been modified, both of these texts yield similar information to similar readers in essentially similar situations. Isn't this a definition of communicative equivalence?

We are not stubbornly committed to the term *equivalence*. A call to abandon the term, however, should be based on more than etymological considerations (Snell-Hornby 1988). No other useful term has been offered in its place. In the context of this volume, the notion of equivalence refers to semantic congruence within the scope of target language prototypical constraints. The source text's textuality is deliberately re-configured to produce a target textuality. There is an intrinsic source text–target text relationship in a good translation that we cannot ignore. If we cannot use the term communicative equivalence to refer to this relationship, what other term would suffice? We will readily adopt a more useful term.

If scholars do not insist on definitions of equivalence that imply complete identity, then equivalence can remain a valid concept in translation studies. There are those who would say that two texts are not equivalent because they are not linguistically identical. Surface-to-surface correspondence is impossible in good translation. Identity disappears at the first transposition. There is a mapping relationship between the source text and target text. This mapping is created by the translator. The semantic congruence of the two texts is achieved by mechanisms that map semantic elements of the L_1 onto structures and sequences in the L_2. A textual segment in the L_2 is presented as a communicative proxy for a structurally different textual segment in the L_1.

Without the notion of communicative equivalence, it is difficult to explain how Japanese computer manuals, which represent a different approach to textualization, can be converted into practical American computer handbooks. As a further example, consider the equivalence of the English translation of the *Swiss Civil Code* to its original (Wyler and Wyler 1987). If English readers in Switzerland read the English text for the same reasons Swiss readers read the Swiss text, aren't the texts communicatively equivalent? These examples argue the case that equivalence in translation cannot be reduced to simple linguistic equivalence. They indicate that equivalence is a measure of how well a text "stands in the place" of another text across cultural and linguistic boundaries. Thus, communicative equivalence and textual equivalence are practical measures of pragmatic and communicative success.

Equivalence is not really a relationship between textual surfaces; it is a relationship of textual effect—of communicative value. Translation scholars cannot decide whether equivalence exists by measuring linguistic correspondence. Translation users measure it by accepting and rejecting translations on the basis of their communicative value.

The issue is not whether linguistic meanings of L_2 items are actually equivalent to L_1 items. It is their textual significance as activators of knowledge which is equivalent. This last notion implies that equivalence can hold between constituent units of texts and not just between texts. The micropropositional structures of a translation are created on the basis of the propositional structures of the source text. They play the same communicative roles in the new text as the parent structures played in the old. Are they not, even conditioned by the target language prototype, communicatively equivalent? The net effect of communicatively equivalent structures acting together in a conventional prototypical framework is communicative equivalence. The translator's recognition of communicative equivalence as an explicit objective is the only mechanism to explain why he or she chooses certain sentence-level renderings in the target text.[70]

When target text micropropositions are given linguistic expression, they are related to the corresponding linguistic expressions in the source text in a more restricted way. Jäger (1975, 145) has termed this relationship *maximal equivalence*. The linguistic surfaces of target sentences possess the greatest equivalence possible at the sentence level.[71] Sentence level concepts of equivalence may be useful in teaching translation, but there is no doubt that serious consideration of the concept of equivalence can only occur beyond the level of individual utterances and sentences (Neubert 1972; Neubert 1973; Jäger and Müller 1982, 45–46).[72] Maximal equivalence, communicative equivalence, and textual equivalence are related but not identical (Neubert 1985). Maximal equivalence expands beyond the sentence boundary to create communicative equivalence. Communicative equivalence becomes textual equivalence at the level of discourse. The concept of *communicative equivalence* provides the bridge between maximal equivalence and textual equivalence. Communicative equivalence in translations is a result of deliberately mediated intertextuality (Van Dijk 1980). An interesting implication of the idea of communicative equivalence is in translation criticism. The user reactions to translations, from complete acceptance to total rejection, could be the basis for an empirical translation criticism.

Communicative equivalence is clearly a central concept for an integrated and interdisciplinary approach to translation because it involves sociolinguistic, linguistic, psychological, critical, and textual issues. It is not a linguistic concept, although it has linguistic ramifications. It involves what has been termed *pragmalinguistics* and *linguistic pragmatics*. The purposes and functions of a translation are decisive factors in creating and evaluating communicative equivalence. Texts are a complex problem-solving strategy evolved to transfer knowledge. Communicative equivalence and textual equivalence can only be understood within individual goal-oriented acts of translation.

We can only understand translation if we understand textuality. We must account for all of the factors that create textual and communicative equivalence between source and target text. There has never been such a thing as the one true translation of a text. Translations do not exist in a social vacuum. An L_1 text has as many translations as there are situations that demand them. Translations prosper in a target culture whose members approach the translation as a resource which can supply valuable aesthetic, practical, and social information. Only the professional translator can produce translations which are the communicative equivalents of source texts. Most students and novices produce texts that are on the fuzzy margins of textuality. Still, even such rough translations may actually suffice, serving a restricted and ephemeral purpose. These wholly linguistic translations force the user to supply all the textual cues that the translator normally provides. The experienced L_2 reader knows what is missing and may have deliberately requested such a non-textual rendering. The greater the cognitive resources of the reader, the fewer the textual cues needed to activate his or her knowledge.

Although most practical translation work strives for communicative equivalence, there are types of translation which do not. *Philological translation* (Reiß 1990, 54) does not try to establish textual equivalence with the world of target texts. This form of translation tries to highlight the semantic and pragmatic uniqueness of the original text. The source text is philologically preserved rather than translated. Most philological translations presume an expectant and expert reader. The retention of source language elements in the target text is deliberate. Philological translation is an exercise in alienation. Such translations are targeted to specific audiences with specific needs and the right backgrounds. Strangely enough, because of the specific intention and discrete situation, these translations might also be considered communicative equivalents. This may expand the notion of communicative equivalence too far. It abandons the relationship of textual meaning to prototypicality which is essential to the notions of communicative and textual equivalence.

Communicative equivalence in translation implies an element of textual indeterminacy. The textual meaning extracted from a text by a reader has been mediated by a translator. That same text may be translated many times, giving rise to alternative L_2 textualizations. There can be many L_2 textualizations, each textually and communicatively equivalent with the source. These alternative textualizations are not, strictly speaking, parallel texts. They share, however, common textual features. They may even contribute to defining one another's textuality. These sibling texts form a translation set, a group of alternative interpretations created under variant communicative conditions.

Text and Translation Theory: An Epilogue

Are there practical implications of the textual approach to translation endorsed in these pages? Consider the ramifications for the teaching of translation (Neubert, 1984). It should be possible to develop pedagogical techniques and resource materials to help student translators become aware of the strategies and tactics of textually aware translation. It would also be useful if the entire range of textuality factors we have described were accounted for in a thorough and detailed syllabus or curriculum. Such a program would be quite useful because it would turn our attention to important empirical questions of predictability and quality control. For instance, are translations that users accept and find useful also translations that exhibit the features of textuality? Quality control is a significant issue in the business of practical translation. Making statements about what translations should look like and about what is wrong with existing translations presupposes an understanding of the factors that create textual and communicative equivalence. By isolating the factors which contribute to equivalence, we can isolate the ways translations go wrong.

The concepts we have presented are an analytic framework which can be used in the empirical study of translation and in translation practice. The conceptual validity and practical utility of our approach can only be tested by the observation of translation practice. Empirical evidence can be used to modify and, if necessary, reject our formulations. We will then have to develop new concepts that account for the observed facts of translation practice. The power that has been claimed for the concept of textual prototypes will take on practical significance, as a pool of empirical knowledge about real texts and real translations is developed to support it. Detailed studies of translations, especially those judged to be successful and effective, are the key to validating the textual approach to translation.

Our arguments also have implications for the old translation concept of translatability. This notion is at the heart of all practical problems of translation. In our view, translatability is determined exclusively by textual considerations. Translatability relies on the potential for textualization and, more broadly, on the potential for communication. The assumption underlying the present investigation is that it is within the text that structured interactions and interactional structures coincide. The discussion has corroborated the claim made by experienced translators and translation scholars that translatability is possible only on textual grounds. Textualization is the global strategy that makes translation possible. Translatability, like communicative equivalence, is a relation between L_1 and L_2 texts. It is only possible within the bounds of their prototypical textuality.[73]

Translators must first and foremost treat a translation as a text. Other models contribute to our understanding of translation as a linguistic, psychological, computational, critical, or social phenomenon. Only the textual approach is completely tied to practice. The idea that translation is a textual process and that a translation is always a text has implications for these other models. The psycholinguistics of translation must deal with processes of text production and comprehension. The sociocultural model must re-evaluate the role of the text as an expression of rule-governed interaction structures and the social relations of textual partners. The limits and future directions of the computational model will be expanded by accounting for textual factors. Even the critical approach unifies with the textual approach at the nexus of the text. Even though we have spoken of the textual process, the end result of the process is a text. The translation result evaluated by the critic is not a random concatenation of decoded and re-encoded linguistic items. It is, or should be, a text in its own right.

Any theory of translation has to account for the textuality of translations. Because a translation is always a text, and because translation is always a textual process, a theory of translation is part of a theory of texts. This volume has proposed a slim outline of a text-based theory of translation. We urge the community of translation scholars to pursue the topics that we have introduced. A text-based theory of translation should be grounded in and verified by the empirical observation and analysis of real texts and real translations. Only then can we come to an understanding of how translation works. With an empirical understanding of the textual process of translation, we can improve the teaching of translation and the practice of translation. Our theory of translation is practice-oriented. It tries to explain and describe translation, but it also aims to improve translation. It will not prescribe how translation should be done. Instead, through the rigorous description of textually and communicatively equivalent translations, it will demonstrate how translation scholarship can be of practical assistance to those presently engaged in studying or practicing one of the most important and most honored professions in the world.[74]

Notes

Preface

1. Reflection on translation is as old as translation itself. Translation has been a topic of interest for both practitioner and theoretician since the times of Ancient Greece. The foundations of many modern approaches to translation can be found in essays and treatises written several centuries ago. Some of these meditations on translation are highly developed considerations of the processes and results of translation. The proponents of modern translation theory should be modest in their claims of originality.
2. See Kuhn's *The Structure of Scientific Revolutions* for an enlightening view of how models and theories develop in the sciences.
3. *Interdiscipline*, as far as we know, was first used in a personal communication from Gideon Toury to Mary Snell-Hornby (Snell-Hornby 1991, 7). It was independently taken up as a frame of reference for the Fifth International Conference on Basic Issues in Translation Studies, in Leipzig, June 25–27, 1991 (Neubert 1993).

Chapter 1

4. We are opposed to the hypothesis that "the basic ability to translate is an innate verbal skill" (Harris and Sherwood 1978, 155). We must also reject the concept of "natural translation" (Harris 1977). The authors follow De Lisle (1988, 20), who clearly distinguishes between bilinguals and professional translators:

> The bilingual generally uses his or her knowledge of a second language to communicate orally; the translator uses texts. Consequently, the translator is never free to express his or her own thoughts. The translator is not free to take liberties with the source text and the original author's ideas.

5. In his most recent attempt to debunk translation theory Newmark (1991, 105–106) writes:

> Translation, I suggest, is a fractured subject which is peculiarly unsuitable for a single integrated theory, a dogma, a blanket statement that will embrace any type of text. In a process and a practice where one often has to think of so many things at the same time ... no one thought-through (*durchdachte*) theory is ever going to cover every translation problem.

Newmark criticizes as many as seven current translation perspectives: functionalist, text-oriented, culture-bound, reception-based, process-centered, communicative, and universalist. He often argues against a model using arguments he has just rejected in another. He closes by expounding his own equally "unified" credo:

> Finally, translation has to be practiced not in the service of the source language text, its traditions, its norms, its culture, nor in the service of the target language text, its smooth conventions, its readerships, its clientele, but critically, sensitively, perceptively, ultimately in the service of universal truths and rights. (1991, 108)

From this formulation one could assume that any translator who attempts to adjust his or her task to a particular kind of text is not serving universal truth. Does this mean that translation scholars should not approach translation studies with a respect for the variety of translation strategy and situation? "Universal truths and rights" are a throwback to the notion of "the one true translation." Who establishes what the truths of translation are? Implicit in this whole formulation is dogma itself. Instead of negating the theoretical contributions of the individual "dogmas," one should respect them as unique perspectives on a complex subject. Only the observation of practice can establish empirical truth.

6. Cf. the formulation of function in Halliday's social semiotic of language: "By a functional theory of language I mean one which attempts to explain linguistic structure, and linguistic phenomena, by reference to the notion that language plays a certain part in our lives; that it is required to serve certain universal types of demand" (Halliday 1971).

7. A previous version of the "model" approach to translation studies appeared in Neubert (1991b). An expanded German version is in Neubert (1992).

8. Berglund (1990, 147) describes three types of source text problems:

1. *Obscurity:* Incorrect or imprecise terminology; syntax and sentence structure so poor that that the intended meaning cannot be discerned; skipped elements in a logical sequence; passages out of context, etc.

2. *Inconsistency:* Lack of terminological stringency; missing information on company preferences; clients' assumptions that the translator will use internal reference materials he is not even told exist, etc.

3. *Interference:* Source texts in a language other than that normally used by the writer are often so structured that they cannot be fully understood without familiarity with the writer's habitual language. Similarly, source texts that have already been translated from another language can be difficult to handle, if they reflect the structure of the original source language.

9. Refer to Neubert (1991b) with a bibliography giving several authors who take this complex grammatico-lexical approach.

10. Within the linguistic model of translation, questions of *equivalence* have been a source of controversy. Equivalence in the linguistic context is a simple correspondence relation. This is what one finds in bilingual dictionaries and in linguistic typology. *Meaning equivalence* is predominantly semantic. It does not account for pragmatics and communicative variables. Since meaning equivalence always relates to issues of language compatibility, it has been a question for linguists since the birth of the discipline. Equivalence has never been interpreted as "meaning identity" by discerning semanticists.

11. Cognitive aspects of interpreting have been a topic of psychological research for some decades (Barik 1970; Gerver and Sinaiko 1977, 1–5, 245–314, 333–342, 385–402). Translation was not put on the psychologist's agenda until quite recently (Danks 1991).

CHAPTER 2

12. "Auf der synchronen Ebene würde der Strukturbegriff—etwa durch das Aufdecken ganz neuer Strukturierungen, wie es heute beispielsweise im Rahmen gesprächsanalytischer Forschungen erfolgt—vielschichtiger werden. So gibt es etwa eine ganze Reihe von Phänomenen in der sprachlichen Kommunikation, die unter dem Blickwinkel eines engen Strukturmodells nichts weiter als Störungen oder Abweichungen (Pausenfüllungen, einige Steuerungssignale, manche Redundanzen usw.), aber unter einem anderen Blickwinkel durchaus funktional sind. Oder es gibt Textabschnitte in mündlicher dialogischer Kommunikation (z.B. 'Sequenzen'), deren Zusammengehörigkeit mit bisherigen Kategorien nicht ohne weiteres und auch nicht befriedigend erklärbar sind, die aber dennoch evidente Struktureinheiten innerhalb von dialogischen Texten darstellen" (Hartung 1981, 1307).

13. Content dominates form in the majority of so-called pragmatic texts. As soon as literary texts are included, this generalization can no longer be made. Fictional texts, although they carry content, derive a significant portion of their meaning from their form.

14. "Translation is an operation performed on languages: a process of substituting a text in one language for a text in another. Clearly, then, any theory of translation must draw upon a theory of language—a general linguistic theory. General linguistics is, primarily, a theory about how languages work" (Catford 1965, 1).

15. The general textual competence of readers and writers may also be joined by special textual competences. These competences, built upon a substrate of general text processing strategies, provide more specific procedures for generating specialized texts. The special competences, such as the ability to produce technical reports or computer manuals, do not develop from the normal stream of textual experience. There is a spectrum of textual abilities, which ranges from the ability to engage in conversation to the ability to write a novel. Only some of these abilities appear through enculturation. The more specialized types require education and special training.

16. Martinet's distinction between first and second articulation with its emphasis on the meaning load of morphemes versus the meaning differentiation of phonemes could be used to postulate a third articulation arising from the function of morphemes and sentences as constituents of textual meaning.

17. I borrow the terminology of Beaugrande and Dressler (1981, 38–45), who present a comprehensive survey of the literature and a useful bibliography.

18. The expression *linguistic item* is taken as a cover term for linguistic signs at various levels of complexity. It includes grammatical and lexical signs up to the level of the utterance.

19. "I remember how I was corrected by a member of the kitchen staff in an Irish college when I asked about the time dinner would be served. She said they did not actually serve dinner but an evening meal and it would be at 6:30 in the evening. My using the term dinner had evidently conveyed to her that I was expecting a three course cooked meal, whereas what she had to offer as the third and last full meal of the day consisted of a variety of salads, cold meat, and only occasionally something cooked. There was never any soup" (Albrecht Neubert, memorat).

20. There may be various reasons for disqualifying *am Boden* as a rendering for *on the ground*. One reason is the metaphorical usage which connotes "in very low spirits" or "down."

21. Cf. ground-ground *Boden-Boden*, ground staff *Bodenpersonal*, ground-to-air *Boden-Bord-*, ground observer *Bodenbeobachter*, ground fog *Bodennebel*, ground forces *Bodentruppen* (as against) *Landstreitkräfte*, air-transmitter *Bordsender*, air-ground *Bord-Boden-*, air-to-air *Bord-zu-Bord*.

22. An exception might be the phrase *keep the change* used by motorists at a gas station.

23. A schema is like a single "scene" from a scenario; a plan is a goal-oriented scenario. A plan is the typical reasoning process which is used to decide a course-of-action. Plans describe the sets of choices that people have to make when they set out to achieve a goal. A "plan is a series of projected actions to realize a goal" (Schank and Abelson 1977, 70–71). Scripts develop out of plans. They "are stabilized plans called up very frequently to specify the roles of participants and their expected actions" (Beaugrande and Dressler 1981, 91).

CHAPTER 3

24. Analyzing textuality poses a methodological problem. All texts are the end products of textuality. The mechanisms for investing knowledge in texts can only be studied using texts that are active in communicative settings. This research problem can be mitigated if the text is artificially projected into a communicative situation. At least this method reminds us that the text is being studied outside of its live communicative context. Providing artificial textual settings is recommended in translation teaching because the problem of using "dead texts" is acute.

25. Her Majesty's Stationery Office, 1954. Later versions exhibit alterations which reflect changes in traffic patterns. They do not invalidate the translation issues.

26. The latest edition of *The Highway Code*, published twenty-four years after the version quoted in the text (1978, reprinted with amendments in 1983), has done away with this pervasive distinction.

27. The problem of translating *realia* is not restricted to quantitative factors. There are more possibilities for recasting their meanings in the L_u than loans and paraphrases. For a thorough analysis and classification of the most suitable translation procedures see Kutz (1977).

28. The problem of what is or what is not required information is dealt with under the textual feature of informativity.

29. A more complete treatment of the constituents of global meaning and the propositional structure of texts is included in the discussion of textual meaning.

30. Other headlines illustrating this habit: Royalty in the red; Tangling by gaslight; Right speaking, wrong reading; An end to innocence; The emperor's new clothes; Rules of the House; Treating like with like; Black notes only; Waving the flag of Hellenism; Where the bora blows; So damned sarcastic; Finishing thought (*Times Literary Supplement*, 12 August 1983).

31. The exception is interpreting, where the sender is usually conscious of the uniqueness of the social setting.

32. The link between situation type and text type is taken up again in the discussion of text types and prototypes.

33. In an earlier attempt to indicate the directedness and relevance of the L_1 text and its translation, this situation type was classified under the heading "pragmatic

types" (Neubert 1968). One reason for reclassifying this important translation phenomenon is the unfortunate vagueness of the concept of pragmatics, which has been used as a cover term for a number of important but heterogeneous phenomena. The concept of situationality provides a more concise basis for classification.

34. The role of situationality in the process of translation was considered more than a hundred years ago by Jacob Grimm. "To translate means to put over, *traducere navem*. Whoever is about to set sail, to man a ship and to take her under full sail across to unknown shores, should not be surprised to arrive in another land where another wind blows" (Albrecht Neubert, trans.).

35. Parallel texts are taken up again in the discussion of translation as result and under intertextuality.

36. For an analysis of the concept of textual "content," read the more complete discussion of textual meaning in Chapter 4.

37. The literature on discourse comprehension is so heterogeneous that it is almost impossible to give an overview. The book by Clark and Clark (1977) attempts a general introduction but is already out of date. A more recent collection of papers is Joshi, Webber, Sag (1981). Another compilation is Just and Carpenter (1977). Text comprehension has become the focus of journals specializing in interdisciplinary approaches to language, witness *Journal of Pragmatics, Text*, and *Discourse Processes*.

38. The notion of an "average" L_1 user is a generalization. There are bound to be gradations of general and special knowledge in the community. The term is used here because of the probability that a core of knowledge about persons, objects, events, states, and processes is shared by all members of a community.

39. For a more detailed discussion of Beaugrande's approach cf. Neubert (1982, 26–33).

40. Schank and Abelson (1977, 12–14) use no more than eleven primitives. They are TRANS, the transfer of an abstract relationship such as possession, ownership, or control (e.g., give, take, buy); PTRANS, the transfer of the physical location of an object (e.g., go); PROPEL, the application of physical force to an object (e.g., push, pull, throw, kick); MOVE, the movement of a body part of an animal by that animal; GRASP, the grasping of an object by an actor (e.g., hold, grab, let go); INGEST, the taking in of an animal or plant to the inside of that animal (e.g., eat, drink, smoke); EXPEL, the expulsion of an object from the body of an animal into the physical world (e.g., sweat, spit, cry); MTRANS, the transfer of mental information between animals or within an animal (e.g., sell, forget); MBUILD, the construction by an animal of new information from old information (e.g., decide, conclude, imagine, consider); SPEAK, the actions of producing sounds (e.g., say, play, music, purr); ATTEND, the action of attending or focusing a sense organ towards a stimulus (e.g., listen, see).

41. Beaugrande (1980a, 79) specifies these four primary concepts as follows: (1) *Objects* are conceptual entities with a stable constitution or identity; (2) *situations* are configurations of objects present and their current states; (3) *events* are occurrences that change a situation or a state within a situation; and (4) *actions* are events intentionally brought about by an agent.

42. The typology offered by Beaugrande (1980a: 81–82) consists of five concept categories of secondary concepts defining the "primary concepts" of events, actions, objects, and situations. Each plays a different defining or specifying role in the textual process.

    A. Defining events, actions, objects, and situations: state, agent, affected entity, relation, attribute, location, time, motion, instrument, form, part, substance, containment, cause, enablement, quantity;

B. Defining human experience: reason, purpose, apperception, cognition, emotion, volition, communication, possession, modality;

C. Defining class inclusion: instance, specification, superclass, metaclass;

D. Defining relations: initiation, termination, entry, exit, proximity, projection;

E. Defining contingencies of symbolic communication: significance, value, equivalence, opposition, co-referentiality, recurrence.

This formulation is in the tradition of earlier attempts to represent the expressiveness of language. The most widely known is *Roget's Thesaurus*. Although Beaugrande (1980a, 78) acknowledges his debt to Roget, this typology and similar recent endeavors by Nida (1975, 178–189) and Wilks (1977) aim to characterize the underlying semantic domains that can be expressed or represented by linguistic means.

43. Re-establishing coherence is an example of how translation is a creative textual act. It cannot be a simple matter of matching. The text is created anew. See Pergnier (1978, 401–451) for a discussion of translation as an ongoing creative process.

44. In the translation of poetry, where formal cohesive devices are an integral part of the message, the situation is different. Linguistic forms that express both semantic and formal relationships must be discovered in the L_2. Although this poses almost insurmountable problems, there is a compensation. Poetry allows for greater freedom in the use and invention of new and unusual collocations and formal devices.

45. The English translation *Leisure and Recreation Activities in the Leipzig Area* was published by the City of Leipzig and printed by DEWAG Leipzig in 1980.

46. Friedrich (1969, 46–50) offers a number of examples illustrating the English preference for hendiadys (double-headed phrases). German favors single-headed phrases with subordinated attributes (e.g., beauty and magic *zauberhafte Schönheit*, individuality and charm *eigener Reiz*, laughter and happiness *glückliches Lachen*, passion and excitement *leidenschaftliche Erregung*, care and attention *sorgfältige Beachtung*).

47. Halliday and Hasan (1976, 288) add "use of the general word" as a fourth type of iteration. This cohesive relation differs from the use of superordinate words only by its greater degree of generality (i.e., book is much more general than novel, dissertation, or treatise; dessert is much more general than cake, fruit-salad, ice cream, or cream puff.

48. Halliday and Hasan (1976, 294): "Properly speaking, reference is irrelevant to lexical cohesion. It is not by virtue of any referential relation that there is a cohesive force set up between two occurrences of a lexical item; rather the cohesion exists as a direct relation between the forms themselves (and thus is more like substitution than reference)."

49. Cf. Neubert (1977, 25–27) where these relations are interpreted in terms of the lexicon and not in terms of the text.

50. "Without our being aware of it, each occurrence of a lexical item carries with it its own textual history, a particular collocational environment that has been built up in the course of the creation of the text and that will provide the context within which the item will be incarnated on this particular occasion. This environment determines the 'instantial meaning,' or text meaning, of the item, a meaning which is unique to each specific instance" (Halliday and Hasan 1976, 289).

51. "A word system is a matrix of words with a common denominator which may be semantic, phonological, etymological, folk-etymological, or associative" (Aphek and Tobin 1981, 32). From the context and from the examples it is clear that word systems

occur in texts and are not to be confused with the concept of "field" in the lexicon (Blanke 1973, 116).

52. The full title is: *Of mice and men and money.* The sub-title is: *Sally Festing visits the Jackson Lab in Bar Harbor, Maine (The Times Higher Education Supplement,* 19 August 1983).

53. In his biography of John Steinbeck, Thomas Kiernan (1979, 208) explains the title as follows:

> Since the dream of George and Lenny (the two main characters of the novel) to acquire their own patch of land was destined to be shattered by the tragic events of which they themselves were to be the unwitting architects, Steinbeck settled on the title 'Of Mice and Men.' It came from Robert Burns' famous phrase, 'The best laid schemes o'mice an' men gang aft a-gley.' The phrase was from a Burns poem that lamented man's enslavement to forces of nature that he cannot control and that relentlessly but indifferently destroy his ambitions and illusions. The title was suggested by Ed Ricketts, a young scientist from Chicago who operated a marine laboratory and biological-supply firm in Monterey, who had led Steinbeck to the Burns poem as an illustration of the scientist's naturalistic and biological determinism. The poem was the quintessence of Rickett's philosophy and it served to recognize and integrate in Steinbeck's mind a number of previously imprecise naturalistic perceptions.

54. Another possibility would be to search for the title of a literary work in the L_2 containing the word *mice.* A suitable title could not be located. One could also select a topic in the text and mention it in the title, as for instance, *2 Millionen Mäuse reichen zur Finanzierung nicht aus.*

55. There is another use of *say,* meaning "say something meaningful," as in *John was talking a lot but not saying much.* Here the sense of the verb justifies the expanded form. *Say* assumes a "fuller" aspectual meaning. The translation poses no problems, since the L_2 (as well as the L_1) has a number of synonyms expressing this semantic variation: *ausdrücken, wirklich sagen.* This distinction is made in the simple form, too: *John talked a lot but said nothing.* The translation of the example, *John redete ständig viel, aber was er dabei sagte, war nicht viel,* also contains anaphoric reference (was) at the level of the complex sentence.

56. Cf. Hopper (1982, 5): "The fundamental notion of aspect is not a local-semantic one but is discourse-pragmatic, and is characterisable as completed event in discourse." In an earlier paper Hopper (1979, 215) speaks of "discourse-conditioned ASPECT" giving examples from Swahili narrative texts. He finds "a tendency . . . for verbs of the durative/stative/iterative to occur in imperfective i.e., backgrounded clauses." This corresponds to our "-ing forms" backgrounding what was previously expressed by punctual verbs with perfective aspect in foregrounded sentences. Backgrounded clauses do not themselves narrate (in our examples, report the news items), but instead they support, amplify, or comment on the narrative (in our examples, situate the news); they "are CONTINGENT and dependent on the story-line events on the content of the news reported" (Hopper 1979, 215–216). He concludes that it is only "from a discursive viewpoint (that) that tense-aspect becomes intelligible" (Hopper 1979, 239).

57. The anaphoric function of the expanded form in English is, of course, not different from the grammatical meanings of individual sentences. The cohesive ties in the newspaper examples are related to the use of the marked form in conversation. "In dialogue the expanded form is usual in statements referring to and commenting on a

particular preceding utterance or action/behavior [e.g.,] I couldn't hope to enjoy myself without you. You're a festivity in yourself. You're making fun of me" (Graustein et al. 1977, 170).

58. This is why the term communicative community is preferred over speech community. A speech community, as the greatest common denominator of those who speak a common language, exists in the form of groups which share certain communicative habits. The expression "communicative community" implies a common linguistic system but also refers to groups of language users who share particular communicative habits.

CHAPTER 4

59. "A 'text type' is a set of heuristics for producing, predicting, and processing textual occurrences, and hence acts as a prominent determiner of efficiency, effectiveness, and appropriateness" (Beaugrande and Dressler 1981, 186). Commenting on these three elements of the type, Beaugrande and Dressler continue (1981, 11), "the *efficiency* of a text depends on its use in communicating with a minimum expenditure of effort by the participants. The *effectiveness* of a text depends on its leaving a strong impression and creating favorable conditions for attaining a goal. The *appropriateness* of a text is the agreement between its setting and the ways in which the standards of textuality are upheld."

60. The use of the term "language" in Marx's dialectical materialist concept of history was developed in *The German Ideology*. It is closely tied to the concrete aims and needs of social groups.

61. A useful attempt to work out a terminological system for textual analysis within the framework of "language as a social semiotic" is Halliday's application of *field, tenor* and *mode*. He expressly restricts the scope of these terms to "the semiotic structure of the situation" (1978, 163–164, 142–145).

62. "Die Sprache ist so alt wie das Bewußtsein die Sprache ist das praktische, auch für andere Menschen existierende, also auch für mich selbst erst existierende wirkliche Bewußtsein und die Sprache entsteht wie das Bewußtsein, erst aus dem Bedürfnis der Notdurft des Verkehrs mit anderen Menschen" (Marx and Engels 1970, 221).

63. In interpreting, the textual meaning of an L_1 text can only be assembled successively. In interpreting, textual meaning is always incomplete. All participants know that they should act accordingly. Nevertheless, after the interpreter has rendered a certain number of passages, he or she is in a position to conceptualize larger portions of meaning (i.e., macrostructural meanings). These conceptualizations will have a bearing on how the remainder of the text will be interpreted.

64. An extreme, but by no means illogical, extension of the textual approach projects the translator's concern well beyond the written text. According to Holz-Mänttäri (1984), it is primarily the "message" (*Botschaft*) and the "assignment", the task the translator was commissioned to fulfill (*Übersetzungsauftrag*), rather than the text itself, that have to be rendered for the "customer". The so-called *skopos* theory of translation (Vermeer 1983; Vermeer 1986), although it does not go as far, derives its impetus from the variable "scope" textual meanings may exhibit in the L_1 and L_2.

65. "It should be recalled that the macrorules are abstract semantic mapping or inference rules and not cognitive rules or strategies. They do not take into account the various cognitive factors that influence the operation of macrorules in discourse comprehension but merely define the linguistic-semantic notion of a 'global meaning' or 'topic' of a discourse" (Van Dijk 1980, 82).

66. Van Dijk makes a further distinction between weak and strong deletion. Weak deletion applies to details of a lower or "local" level of the discourse. Strong deletion refers to semantic material which is left out at a much more global level (Van Dijk 1980, 47).

67. Cf. Jäger (1983, 55–57) who discusses the components of the communicative value of a text or utterance.

68. Of course, complete identity is also not achieved in monolingual communication. The factors influencing the process of communication can never be kept constant between sender and receiver. The participants introduce their unique social and individual communicative histories into the interactive situation.

69. This is, in fact, Van Dijk's definition of cognitive set.

70. If someone changes the mode of address from *Sie* to *du* in a German novel, the distinction is usually important for the plot. The English rendering of the microstructure in which this occurs, which cannot be expressed by the same grammatical means, is of paramount importance for the global meaning of the L_2 text. A failure to solve this microsemantic equivalence problem would have repercussions for the communicative value of the text as a whole.

71. This critique of translation studies is, in our view, misguided. In his generally useful book, *The Translator's Turn*, Robinson (1991) rejects modern translation studies because, in his view, it relies too heavily on static linguistic correspondences. He claims that given "the dominant logical tradition of Western thought it is, perhaps, only to be expected that translation theory should set on static ideals of structural equivalence for translation quality or success." Robinson is referring to a very mechanical process of translation that does not exist in the profession or in the translation classroom. He continues:

> two texts, SL and TL, are placed side by side or superimposed like transparencies, the 'feel' of the language used fading away like a dream, leaving only the bare bone of lexical, syntactic, and semantic structures then checked for correspondences. And where structural correspondence is king, it is, again, only to be expected that the translator be conceived as a mechanical device for the achievement of equivalence a human being, to be sure, but one who must not draw on the full creative range of his or her humanity, must not access emotional predilections or associations, indeed must access only the most carefully controlled and circumscribed sort of linguistic expertise, exposure to the logical system underlying everyday speech. (Robinson 1991, 113–134)

While we agree with this condemnation of linguistic translation, Robinson's description does not coincide with the wide range of translation theory. It is clear that Robinson is somewhat isolated from the main thrust of international translation theory. The situation he describes has not existed since well before the *pragmatische Wende* of the seventies. This isolation is typical of "indigenous" translation studies in the United States. Compare Alan Melby's paper at the 1989 Montreal Conference where a convincing and cogent argument was delivered a decade too late. This situation is partly due to the fragmented nature of American translation studies, its subjugation to traditional language departments, its tangential relationship to the translating profession, and the fact that many seminal works in the field are not available in English.

72. Jäger and Müller (1982) make a valid point when they conclude that L_2 texts which do not satisfy the criterion of maximal equivalence might not be termed translations at all. These texts may be perfectly justified by the social practice of bilingually mediated communication (*Sprachmittlung*), but should perhaps be called adaptations that exhibit *communicative heterovalence* (Jäger and Müller 1982, 55–56; Jäger 1980).

73. One could imagine that a communicative community does not include in its textual repertoire a prototype which is well developed in another community (advertising texts among the Australian aborigines). This is a case of genuine intranslatability. The history of translation, however, has many examples where intranslatability has given way under the impact of social and communicative needs developed under the direct influence of language contact.

74. Goethe in a letter to Thomas Carlyle: "Was man auch von der Unzulänglichkeit des Übersetzens sagen mag, so ist und bleibt es doch eines der wichtigsten und würdigsten Geschäfte in dem gesamten Weltwesen" (Goethe 1907).

References

Anderson, J. R. 1976. *Language, Memory, and Thought.* Hillsdale N.J.: Erlbaum.
Aphek, E., and Y. Tobin. 1981. Problems in the Translation of Word Systems. *Journal of Literary Semantics* 10(1):32–43.
———. 1983. The Means is the Message: On the Intranslatability of a Hebrew Text. *Meta* 28(1):57–69.
Austin, J. 1962. *How to Do Things with Words.* London: Oxford University Press.
Barik, H. C. "A Study of Simultaneous Interpretation." Ph.D. diss., University of North Carolina at Chapel Hill, 1970.
Barnhart, C. L., S. Steinmetz, and R. K. Barnhart. 1980. *The Second Barnhart Dictionary of New English.* Bronxville, N.Y.: Barnhart Books.
Barthes, R. 1979. From Word to Text. In *Textual Strategies,* ed. J. Harari, 73–81. Ithaca: Cornell University Press.
Beaugrande, R. de. 1978. *Factors in a Theory of Poetic Translation.* Assen: van Gorcum.
———. 1980a. *Text, Discourse, and Process.* London: Longman.
———. 1980b. Towards a Semiotic Theory of Literary Translating. In *Semiotik und Übersetzen,* ed. W. Wills, 23–42. Tübingen: Narr.
Beaugrande, R. de, and W. Dressler. 1981. *Introduction to Text Linguistics.* London: Longman.
Berglund, L. O. 1990. The Search for Social Significance. *Lebende Sprachen* 35(4): 145–51.
Bickerton, D. 1973. The Structure of Polylectal Grammars. In *Sociolinguistics: Current Trends and Prospects,* ed. R. Shuy, 17–42. Washington, D.C.: Georgetown University Press.
Bierwisch, M. 1979. Wörtliche Bedeutung-eine pragmatische Gretchenfrage. *Linguistische Studien* Reihe A(60):48–80.
Blanke, G. 1973. *Einführung in die semantische Analyse.* Munich: Hueber.
Bobrow, D., and A. Collins, eds. 1975. *Representation and Understanding.* New York: Academic Press.
Bobrow, D., and T. Winograd. 1977. An Overview of KRL: A Knowledge Representation Language. *Cognitive Science* 1:3–46.
Bouchard, J. 1960. *The Twin-Bed Marketing Technique.* Quebec: Editions Belle Province.
Bühler, H. 1988. Introductory Paper: Text Linguistics, Text Types and Prototypes. *Meta* 33(4):465–67.
Catford, J. C. 1965. *A Linguistic Theory of Translation.* London: Oxford University Press.
Clark, H., and E. Clark. 1977. *Language and Psychology.* New York: Harcourt, Brace and Jovanovich.

Clark, H., and C. R. Marshall. 1981. Definite Reference and Mutual Knowledge. In *Elements of Discourse Understanding*, ed. A. Joshi, B. Webber, and I. Sag, 10–63. London: Cambridge University Press.
Cresswell, M. J., 1973. *Logic and Languages*. London: Methuen.
Danks, J. 1993. The Psycholinguistics of Reading and Translation. In *Proceedings of the Fifth International Conference on Basic Issues in Translation Studies*, ed. G. Shreve, A. Neubert, and K. Gommlich. Kent State University Forum on Translation Studies no. 2. Kent, Ohio.
DeLisle, J. 1980. *Translation: An Interpretive Approach*. Translation Studies, no. 8. London: University of Ottawa Press.
Dillon, G. 1982. *Constructing Texts: Elements of a Theory of Composition and Style*. Bloomington: Indiana University Press.
Duff, A. 1981. *The Third Language: Recurrent Problems of Translation into English*. Oxford, New York: Pergamon.
Eikmeyer, H. J. 1983. Procedural Analysis of Discourse. *Text* 3(3):11–37.
Fillmore, C. J. 1976. Frame Semantics and the Nature of Language. *Annals of the New York Academy of Science* 280:20–31.
Fishman, J. A. 1968. *Readings in the Sociology of Language*. The Hague: Mouton.
Friedrich, W. 1969. *Technik des Übersetzens, Englisch und Deutsch*. Munich: Hueber.
Garnham, A. 1983. What's Wrong with Story Grammars. *Cognition* 15:145–54.
Garnham, A., J. Oakhill, and P. N. Johnson-Laird. 1982. Referential Continuity and the Coherence of Discourse. *Cognition* 11:29–46.
Gerver, D., and H. W. Sinaiko. 1977. *Language Interpretation and Communication*. New York and London: Plenum.
Goethe, W. 1907. *Goethes Werke*. Weimar: Böhlaus.
Goldman, S. R. 1982. Knowledge Systems for Realistic Goals. *Discourse Processes* 5(34):279–304.
Gommlich, K., and K. Förster. 1991. Text Patterns in a Computer-assisted Translation System. *Linguistische Studien* A(196):72–79.
Graustein, G. et al. 1977. *English Grammar: A University Handbook*. Leipzig: Enzyklopädie.
Greimas, A. J., and J. Courtes. 1982. *Semiotics and Language: An Analytical Dictionary*. Bloomington: Indiana University Press.
Grice, P. 1975. Logic and Conversation. In *Speech Acts*, ed. E. P. Cox and J. L. Morgan, 41–48. Syntax and Semantics, vol. 3. New York, San Francisco, London: Academic Press.
Gumperz, J. 1982. *Discourse Strategies: Studies in Interactional Sociolinguistics*. Cambridge: Cambridge University Press.
Gutt, E. A. 1990. A Theoretical Account of Translation—Without a Translation Theory. *Target* 2(2):135–64.
Hall, E. T. 1959. *The Silent Language*. Greenwich, Conn.: Fawcett.
Halliday, M. A. K. 1971. Linguistic Function and Literary Style: an Inquiry into the Language of William Golding's *The Inheritors*. In *Literary Style: A Symposium*, ed. S. Chatman, 362–400. New York: Oxford University Press.
———. 1978. *Language as a Social Semiotic*. London: Arnold.
Halliday, M. A. K., and R. Hasan. 1976. *Cohesion in English*. London: Longman.
Harris, B. 1977. The Importance of Natural Translation. *Working Papers on Bilingualism* 12:96–114.
———. 1983a. Translation, Translation Teaching, and the Transfer of Technology. *Meta* 28(1):5–16.

———. 1983b. Co-writing: A Canadian Technique of Communicative Equivalence. In *Semantik und Übersetzungswissenschaft*, ed. G. Jäger and A. Neubert, 121–32. Übersetzungswissenschaftliche Beiträge 6. Leipzig: Verlag Enzyklopädie.
Harris, B., and B. Sherwood. 1978. Translating as an Innate Skill. In *Language, Interpretation, and Communication*, eds. D. Gerver and H. W. Sinaiko, 155–70. New York and London: Plenum.
Harris, Z. S. 1963. *Discourse Analysis Reprints*. The Hague: Mouton.
Hartmann, R. R. K. 1980. *Contrastive Textology: Comparative Discourse Analysis in Applied Linguistics*. Heidelberg: Groos.
Hartung, W. 1981. Über die Gesellschaftlichkeit der Sprache. *Deutsche Zeitschrift für Philosophie* 8:1302-14.
Hasan, R. 1968. *Part I: Grammatical Cohesion in Spoken and Written English*. Papers of the Programme in Linguistics and English Teaching Series I, vol. 7. London: Longman.
Hintikka, K. J. J. 1962. *Knowledge and Belief*. Ithaca: Cornell University Press.
Holz-Mänttäri, J. 1984. *Translatorisches Handeln: Theorie und Methode*. Helsinki: Suomalainen Tiedeakatemia.
Hopper, Paul J. 1979. Aspect and Foregrounding in Discourse. In *Discourse and Syntax*, ed. T. Givon, 213–41. *Syntax and Semantics*, vol. 12. New York: Academic Press.
———. 1982. *Tense-aspect Between Semantics and Pragmatics*. Amsterdam: Benjamins.
Hymes, D. 1962. The Ethnography of Speaking. In *Anthropology and Human Behavior*, ed. T. Gladwin and W. C. Sturtevant, 99–138. Washington D.C.: Anthropological Society of Washington.
Jäger, G. 1975. *Translation und Translationslinguistik*. Halle: Niemeyer.
———. 1980. Translation und Adaptation. *Linguistische Arbeitsberichte* 26:1–11.
———. 1983. Theorie der sprachlichen Bedeutungen und Translation. In *Semantik und Übersetzungswissenschaft*, ed. G. Jäger and A. Neubert, 53–61. Übersetzungswissenschaftliche Beiträge 6. Leipzig: Verlag Enzyklopädie.
Jäger, G., and D. Müller. 1982. Kommunikative und Maximale Äquivalenz von Texten. In *Äquivalenz bei der Translation*, ed. G. Jäger and A. Neubert, 43–57. Übersetzungswissenschaftliche Beiträge 5. Leipzig: Verlag Enzyklopädie.
Jäger, G., and A. Neubert, A. 1982. *Äquivalenz bei der Translation*. Übersetzungswissenschaftliche Beiträge 5, Leipzig: Enzyklopädie.
Johnson-Laird, P. N. 1981. Mental Models of Meaning. In *Elements of Discourse Understanding*, ed. A. Joshi, B. Webber, and I. Sag, 106–26. London: Cambridge University Press.
Joshi, A., B. Webber, and I. Sag. 1981. *Elements of Discourse Understanding*. Cambridge: Cambridge University Press.
Just, M. A. and Carpenter, P. A. 1977. *Cognitive Processes in Comprehension*. New York: Erlbaum.
Kelletat, A. F. 1987. Die Rückschritte der Übersetzungstheorie. In *Übersetzen im Fremdsprachenunterricht: Beiträge zu Übersetzungswissenschaft—Annäherunen an eine Übersetzungsdidaktik*, ed. R. Ehnert and W. Schleyer, 33–49. Materialien Deutsch als Fremdsprache vol. 26. Regensburg: Johannes-Gutenberg Universität.
Kiernan, T. 1979. *The Intricate Music: A Biography of John Steinbeck*. Boston, Toronto: Little, Brown.
Kintsch, W. 1977. *Memory and Cognition*. New York: Wiley.
Krings, H. P. 1986a. Was in den Köpfen von Übersetzern vorgeht. Eine empirische Untersuchung zur Struktur des Übersetzungsprozesses an fortgeschrittenen Französichelernern. *Tübinger Beiträge zur Linguistik* 291.

———. 1986b. Translation Problems and Translation Strategies of Advanced German Learners of French. In *Interlingual and Intercultural Communication: Discourse and Cognition in Translation and Second Language Acquisition Studies*, ed. J. House and S. Blum-Kulka, 263–75. Tübingen: Narr.

———. 1988. Blick in die 'Black Box'—Eine Fallstudie zum Übersetzungsprozeß bei Berufsübersetzern. In *Textlinguistik und Fachsprache: Akten des Internationalen Übersetzungswissenschaftlichen AILA-Symposium*, ed. R. Arntz, 393–412. Hildesheim: Olms.

Kuhn, T. S. 1970. *The Structure of Scientific Revolutions*. Chicago: University of Chicago Press.

Kutz, V. 1977. Zur translatorischen Auflösung der Nulläquivalenz russischsprachiger Realienlexeme im Deutschen. Diss. A, Karl-Marx-Universität, Leipzig.

Labov, W. 1970. The Study of Language in its Social Contexts. *Studium Generale* 23:30–87.

Lawson, V. 1983. The Language of Patents. A Typology of Patents, with Particular Reference to Machine Translation. *Lebende Sprachen* 2:58–61.

Lewis, D. K. 1969. *Convention*. Cambridge: Harvard University Press.

Lyons, J. 1977. *Semantics: Volume I*. Cambridge: Cambridge University Press.

Mandler, J. M., and N. S. Johnson. 1977. Remembrance of Things Passed: Story Structure and Recall. *Cognitive Psychology* 9:111–51.

Martinet, A. 1964. *Eléments de linguistique générale*. Paris: Librairie Armand Colin.

Marx, K., and F. Engels. 1970. *Die deutsche Ideologie*. Marx und Engels, Ausgewählte Werke vol. 1. Berlin: Dietz

Meyer, B. 1975. *The Organization of Prose and its Effects on Memory*. Amsterdam: North Holland.

Miller, J. States of Mind: Conversation with Psychological Investigators, BBC Radio Interview. London, 1983.

Mitchell, T. F. 1984. Soziolinguistische und stilistische Aspekte des gesprochenen Arabisch der Gebildeten Educated Spoken Arabic in Ägypten und der Levante. *Sitzungsberichte der Sächsischen Akademie der Wissenschaften zu Leipzig* 123(6): 228–40.

Neubert, A. 1968a. *Grundfragen der Übersetzungswissenschaft*. Fremdsprachen, Beiheft II. Leipzig: Verlag Enzyklopädie.

———. 1968b. Pragmatische Aspekte der Übersetzung. In *Grundfragen der Übersetzungswissenschaft*, ed. A. Neubert. Fremdsprachen, Beiheft II. Leipzig: Verlag Enzyklopädie.

———. 1972. Theorie und Praxis für die Übersetzungswissenschaft. In *Applied Contrastive Linguistics, Proceedings of the Third AILA Congress Copenhagen*, 38–60. Heidelberg: Groos.

———. 1973a. Invarianz und Pragmatik. In *Neue Beiträge zu Grundfragen der Übersetzungswissenschaft II*, ed. A. Neubert and O. Kade, 13–26. Leipzig: Enzyklopädie.

———. 1973b. Zur Determination des Sprachsystems. *Zeitschrift für Phonetik, Sprachwissenschaft und Kommunikationsforschung* 26(6):617–29.

———. 1979. Words and Texts. *Linguistische Studien* Reihe A(55):16–29.

———. 1980. Textual Analysis and Translation Theory, or What Translators Should Know about Texts. *Linguistische Arbeitsberichte* 38:23–31.

———. 1982. Textsemantische Bedingungen für die Translation. *Äquivalenz bei der Translation*, ed. G. Jäger and A. Neubert, 22–36. Übersetzungswissenschaftliche Beiträge 5. Leipzig: Verlag Enzyklopädie.

———. 1983a. Translation und Texttheorie. In *Semantik und Übersetzungswissenschaft*, ed. G. Jäger and A. Neubert, 100–110. Übersetzungswissenschaftliche Beiträge 6. Leipzig: Verlag Enzyklopädie.

———. 1983b. Methodologische Aspekte des Verhältnisses zwischen Konfrontations- und Translationslinguistik. In *Studien zur Sprachkonfrontation Englisch-Deutsch*, ed. K. Hansen, 32–34. Berlin: Humboldt-Universität.

———. 1984. Text-bound Translation Teaching and the Prototype View. In *Die Theorie des Übersetzens und ihr Aufschlußwert für die Übersetzungs- und Dolmetschdidaktik*, ed. W. Wills and G. Thome, 61–70. Proceedings of the International Association for Applied Linguistics. Tübingen: Narr.

———. 1985a. Maximale Äquivalenz auf Textebene? *Linguistische Arbeitsberichte* 47: 12–23.

———. 1985b. Textlinguistik des Übersetzens. *Linguistische Studien* Reihe A(135): 15–24.

———. 1986. Translatorische Relativität. In *Übersetzungswissenschaft—eine Neuorientierung. Zur Integrierung von Theorie und Praxis*, ed. M. Snell-Hornby, 8-105. Tübingen: Francke.

———. 1987. Beziehungen zwischen Semantik und Pragmatik in translatorischer Sicht. *Sitzungsberichte der Akademie der Wissenschaften der DDR* 15:40–44.

———. 1988. Top-down Prozeduren bei translatorischen Informationstransfer. In *Semantik, Kognition und Äquivalenz*, ed. G. Jäger and A. Neubert, 18–30. Übersetzungs wissenschaftliche Beiträge 11. Leipzig: Enzyklopädie.

———. 1989. Interference Between Languages and Between Texts. In *Interferenz in der Translation*, ed. H. Schmidt, 56–64. Übersetzungswissenschaftliche Beiträge 12. Leipzig: Enzyklopädie.

———. 1990. Übersetzen als Aufhebung des Ausgangstextes. In *Übersetzungswissenschaft, Ergebnisse und Perspektiven. Festschrift für Wolfram Wilss zum 65. Geburtstag*, ed. R. Arntz and G. Thome, 31–39. Tübingen: Narr.

———. 1991a. Computed-Aided Translation: Where are the Problems. *Target* 3(1): 55–64.

———. 1991b. Models of Translation. In *Empirical Research in Translation and Intercultural Studies. Selected Papers of the TRANSIF Seminar*, ed. S. Tirkonnen-Condit, 17–26. Tübingen: Narr.

———. 1992. Alternative Modelle des Übersetzens. In *Fremdsprachenunterricht im internationalen Vergleich-Perspektive 2000*, ed. C. Gnutzmann, F. Königs and W. Pfeiffer. Reihe Schule und Forschung. Frankfurt: Diesterweg. In print.

———. 1993. Introduction to the Fifth International Conference on Basic Issues in Translation Studies. In *Proceedings of the Fifth International Conference on Basic Issues in Translation Studies*, ed. G. Shreve, A. Neubert, and K. Gommlich. Kent State University Forum on Translation Studies no. 2. Kent, Ohio. Forthcoming.

Newell, A., and H. Simon. 1972. *Human Problem Solving*. Englewood Cliffs: Prentice Hall.

Newmark, P. 1981. *Approaches to Translation*. Oxford, New York: Pergamon.

———. 1983. Translation and the Informative Function of Language. *Lebende Sprachen* 28(4):160–65.

———. 1989. Modern Translation Theory. *Lebende Sprachen* 34(1):6–9.

———. 1991. The Curse of Dogma in Translation Studies. *Lebende Sprachen* 36(3): 105–8.

Nida, E. A. 1975. *Componential Analysis of Meaning*. The Hague: Mouton.

Nida, E. A., and C. Taber. 1969. *The Theory and Practice of Translation*. Leiden: Brill.

Norton, G. P. 1984. *The Ideology and Language of Translation in Renaissance France and their Human Antecedents.* Geneva: Droz.
Omanson, R. C. 1982. An Analysis of Narratives: Identifying Central Supportive, and Distracting Content. *Discourse Processes* 5(34):195–224.
Pergnier, M. 1978. *Les fondements sociolinguistiques de la traduction.* Paris: Diffusion Librairie Honoré Champion.
Perret, J. 1975. Traduction et paroles. In *Problèmes de la traduction littéraire.* Louvain: Bibliothèque de l'Université.
Petöfi, J. S. 1979. *Text vs. Sentence: Basic Questions of Text Linguistics.* Hamburg: Buske.
———. 1983. *Methodological Aspects of Discourse Processing.* Text, vol. 6, no. 1. Amsterdam: Mouton.
Reiß, K. 1990. Das Mißverständnis vom "eigentlichen" Übersetzen. In *Übersetzungswissenschaft: Ergebnisse und Perspektiven. Festschrift für Wolfram Wilss zum 65. Geburtstag,* ed. R. Arntz and G. Thome, 40–54. Tübingen: Narr.
Reiß, K., and H. Vermeer. 1984. *Grundlegung einer allgemeinen Translationstheorie.* Tübingen: Niemeyer.
Robinson, D. 1991. *The Translator's Turn.* Baltimore and London: Johns Hopkins University Press.
Rumelhart, D. E. 1975. Notes on a Schema for Stories. In *Representation and Understanding,* ed. D. G. Bobrow and A. Collins, 211–36. New York: Academic Press.
Saussure, F. de. 1916. *Cours de Linguistique Générale.* Paris: Payot.
Savory, T. 1968. *The Art of Translation.* 2nd ed. London: Cape.
Schank, R. 1975. *Conceptual Information Processing.* Amsterdam: North Holland.
———. 1982. *Dynamic Memory. A Theory of Reminding and Learning in Computers and People.* Cambridge: Cambridge University Press.
Schank, R., and R. Abelson. 1977. *Scripts, Plans, Goals and Understanding. An Inquiry in Human Knowledge Structures.* Hillsdale, N.J.: Erlbaum.
Schank, R., and J. R. Carbonell. 1979. Re: The Gettysburg Address: Representing Social and Political Acts. In *Associative Networks,* ed. N. V. Findler, 327–62. London: Academic Press.
Scherf, W. 1990. Computer-assisted Translation, the Workstation, and the Translator. In *TKE '90: Terminology and Knowledge Engineering Volume I,* ed. H. Czap and W. Nedobity, 574–78. Frankfurt: Indeks Verlag.
Schmidt, H. 1982. Zur Beschreibung der Äquivalenzbeziehungen bei Kompressionen in Übersetzungen aus dem Russischen ins Deutsche. Diss. B., Karl-Marx-Universität, Leipzig.
Schutz, A. 1963. Concept and Theory Formation in the Social Sciences. In *Philosophy of the Social Sciences,* ed. M. Natanson. New York: Random House.
———. 1970. *On Phenomenology and Social Relations.* Chicago: Chicago University Press.
Sdun, W. 1967. *Probleme und Theorien des Übersetzens in Deutschland vom 18. bis zum 20. Jahrhundert.* Munich: Hueber.
Séguinot, T. C. 1982. The Editing Function of Translation. *Bulletin of the Canadian Association of Applied Linguistics* 4(1):151–61.
Shreve, G. M. 1990. Requirements Analysis, Empirical Research and Prototyping in the Software Engineering of Workstations for Computer-Assisted Translation. In *TKE '90: Terminology and Knowledge Engineering Volume I,* ed. H. Czap and W. Nedobity, 553–64. Frankfurt: Indeks Verlag.
———. 1991. Evolution of the Translator's Workstation as Virtual Desktop: Software Services and User Environment. In *Proceedings of the 32nd Annual Conference of the American Translators Association,* ed. L. Willson, 307–16. Medford: Learned Information Inc.

Shreve, G. M., C. Schäffner, J. Danks, and J. Griffin. 1992. Is There a Special Kind of Reading For Translation? An Empirical Study of the Role of Reading in Translation. Kent State University Institute for Applied Linguistics.

Smith, N. V. 1982. *Mutual Knowledge*. London, New York: Academic Press.

Snell-Hornby, M. 1986. Übersetzen, Sprache, Kultur. *Übersetzungswissenschaft eine Neuorientierung. Zur Integrierung von Theorie und Praxis*, 9–29. Tübingen: Francke.

———. 1988. *Translation Studies. An Integrated Approach*. Amsterdam and Philadelphia: John Benjamins.

———. 1991. Übersetzungswissenschaft: Eine neue Disziplin für eine alte Kunst? *BDÜ Mitteilungsblatt für Übersetzer und Dolmetscher* 37(1):4–10.

Sperber, D., and D. Wilson. 1982. Mutual Knowledge and Relevance in Theories of Comprehension. In *Mutual Knowledge*, ed. N. V. Smith, 61–100. London, New York: Academic Press.

Stein, N. L. 1982. What's in a Story: Interpreting in Interpretation of Story Grammars. *Discourse Processes* 5(34):319–35.

Sutherland, D. 1983. Taking the Lid off the Brain. *The Times Literary Supplement*, June 17, 641.

Talentino, K. 1991. The Translation of Spanish Medical Texts. Master's thesis, Kent State University, Kent, Ohio.

Thorndike, P. 1977. Cognitive Structures in Comprehension and Memory of Narrative Discourses. *Cognitive Psychology* 9:77–100.

Toury, G. 1982. A Rationale for Descriptive Translation Studies. *Disposition* 7(20): 23–39.

Van Dijk, T. A. 1980. *Macrostructures, An Interdisciplinary Study of Global Structures in Discourse, Interaction, and Cognition*. Hillsdale, N.J.: Erlbaum.

Vázquez-Ayora, G. 1977. *Introducción a la Traductología*. Georgetown: Georgetown University Press.

Venuti, L. 1986. The Translator's Invisibility. *Criticism* 28(2):179–212.

———. 1991. Translation as A Social Practice; or, The Violence of Translation. Paper presented at conference, Humanistic Dilemmas: Translation in the Humanities and Social Sciences, 26–28 September, at the State University of New York, Binghamton, New York.

Vermeer, H. 1983. Aufsätze zur Translationstheorie. Heidelberg: N.p.

———. 1986. Voraussetzungen für eine Translationstheorie. Heidelberg: N.p.

Wilks, Y. 1977. Good and Bad Arguments about Semantic Primitives. *Communication and Cognition* 10:181–221.

Winograd, T. 1975. Frame Representations and the Declarative Procedural Controversy. In *Representation and Understanding*, ed. D. Bobrow and A. Collins, 185–210. New York: Academic Press.

Winston, P. 1977. *Artificial Intelligence*. Reading, Mass.: Addison, Wesley.

Woods, W. A. 1981. Procedural Semantics as a Theory of Meaning. In *Elements of Discourse Understanding*, ed. A. Joshi, B. Webber, and I. Sag, 300–334. London: Cambridge University Press.

Wyler, S., and B. Wyler, trans. 1987. *The Swiss Civil Code*. Oxford: Oxford University Press.

Index

Aphek, E., 110, 154n. 51

Barik, H. C., 151n. 11
Barnhart, C. L., 67
Beaugrande, R. de, 83, 86, 87, 90, 93, 95, 97, 99, 117, 118, 151n. 17, 152n. 23, 153nn. 41, 42, 154n. 42
Berglund, L. O., 17, 22, 150n. 8
Bickerton, D., 39
Blanke, G., 154–55n. 51
Bobrow, D., 49
Bouchard, J., 84
Bühler, H., 134

Catford, J. C., 20, 44, 151n. 14
Clark, E., 153n. 37
Clark, H., 54, 55, 56, 59, 153n. 37
Cognitive set, 141
Coherence, 93–102
  determiners of, 95–98
  global, 100–102
  logical structure of, 96–97, 107
  typology of markers of, 98–100
Cohesion, 102–16
  by collocation, 104–9
  grammatical, 113–17
  hyponymic, 106
  interference, 104
  by iteration, 108–9
  lexical, 104–13, 116
  polyvalent, 112
Communicative value, 24, 140–42
  and heterovalence, 140–41, 157n. 72
Community co-membership, 55

Concepts in texts
  primary, 99, 153–54n. 42
  secondary, 99, 153–54n. 42
Conceptual dependency theory, 99
Copresence, 56–59
  direct, 58
  immediate, 56
  indirect, 58–59
  linguistic, 57–59, 128
  potential physical, 57
  prior physical, 56
  understandability as precondition for, 57
Correspondence rules, 19, 44
Co-writing, 84
Cresswell, M. J., 78

Danks, J., 50, 151n. 11
Dead texts, 152n. 24
De Lisle, J., 149n. 4
Displaced interaction, 37
Dressler, W., 83, 86, 87, 90, 93, 117, 118, 151n. 17, 152n. 23, 156n. 59
Duff, A., 117

Eikmeyer, H. J., 45
Equivalence, 143–46, 150n. 10
  communicative, 142–46
  maximal, 144–45
  textual, 142–46

Fillmore, C., 60–64
Frames, 60–65, 105

166

cognitive, 60–61
correspondence of, 64
criterial, 63
extension of, 67
interactional, 62
programmed, 66–67
textual references to, 65
Friedrich, W., 154n. 46

Garnham, A., 127
Gerver, D., 151n. 11
Gommlich, K., 28
Graustein, G., 113, 155–56n. 57
Grice, P., 75, 77, 79, 82–84
Gumperz, J., 126, 129
Gutt, E. A., 138

Hall, E. T., 61
Halliday, M. A. K., 102, 104, 108, 116, 150n. 6, 154n. 47, 156n. 61
Harris, B., 84, 122, 149n. 4
Hartung, W., 40, 151n. 12
Hintikka, K. J. J., 78
Holz-Mänttäri, J., 74, 156n. 64
Hopper, P. J., 155n. 56

Interactional aim, 71, 112
Intertextuality, 117–23
    mediated, 118–20

Jäger, G., 20, 144, 157n. 72
Johnson-Laird, P. N., 95

Knowledge
    broker, 34
    mutual, 53–56
    procedural, 45
Krings, H. P., 30, 31
Kuhn, T. S., 149n. 2
Kutz, V., 152n. 27

Labov, W., 39
Language mediation, 1
Lawson, V., 86

Lewis, D. K., 54
Lexical field, 103
Lyons, J., 78

Macroprocessing, 141
Macroproposition, 137–38
Macrorule, 137–40
    construction, 139
    deletion, 138
    generalization, 138
    zero, 138
Macrostructure, 137–40
Martinet, 151n. 16
Maxim of manner, 82–84
Maxim of quality, 77
Maxim of quantity, 75
Maxim of relation, 79
Meaning invariance, 21
Melby, A., 157n. 71
Meyer, B., 46
Microproposition, 137–38
Microstructure, 137–40
Miller J., 48
Mitchell, T. F., 39

Neubert, A., 23, 24, 29, 44, 75, 109, 118, 119, 134, 137, 144, 146, 149, 150nn. 7, 9, 152–53n. 33, 154n. 49
Newmark, P., 14, 22, 32, 78, 83, 117, 149n. 5
Nida, E., 117, 154n. 42

Pergnier, M., 154n. 43
Plans, 66, 68, 152n. 23
Possible world, 59, 78–79
Principle of cooperation, 74
Prototype, 130–35
    analysis, 134–35
    as fuzzy type, 131
    and textuality, 133
    superstructure, 133
Pseudo-collocation, 104

Realia, 76
Reiß, K., 77, 145

INDEX / 167

Retextualization, 7, 134
Robinson, D., 157n. 71

Savory, T., 9
Scenario, 66–68
Schank, R., 98, 99, 152n. 23, 153n. 40
Schema, 66, 68, 152n. 23
Scherf, W., 28
Schmidt, H., 76
Schutz, A., 32, 42, 66
Script, 66, 68, 152n. 23
Séguinot, C., 87–88
Semantic quanta, 21
Shreve, G., 28, 50, 90
Situation
  adaptation in translation, 88
  equivalence of, 88
  management, 86
  types, 86
Skopos theory, 156n. 64
Smith, N. V., 54
Snell-Hornby, M., 33, 134, 142, 143, 149n. 3
Social course-of-action, 42, 52–53, 66
Source text deficiency, 17
Speech community, 55
Sperber, D., 56
Stein, N. L., 128

Talentino, K., 122
Text
  abstract, 67
  global meaning of, 23, 138–40
  global proposition of, 137–38
  grammar, 40
  heuristic, 90
  ideological, 26
  as interaction structure, 39
  mental model of, 14, 15, 23, 95, 136
  native, 89
  optimal, 83
  parallel, 89–90, 118, 137
  type, 120, 125–30, 156n. 59
  world, 41
Text processing, 44
  comprehension, 48–49
  production, 45–49

Text typology, 125–30
  first-order, 42, 123, 126–27, 130
  second-order, 123, 126–27, 133
Text-induced text production, 25, 43, 119
Textness, 69–70, 135
Textonymy, 109–12
Textual
  acceptability, 18, 73–84
  competence, 45–46
  conventions, 118
  expectation, 42, 118–20, 126–27
  informativity, 88–93
  intentionality, 70–73
  —productive, 71
  —receptive, 72, 80
  markers, 128–30
  meaning, 135–37
  order of informativity, 90–91
  profile, 42, 117
  relevance, 72, 79–82, 91
  situationality, 84–88
  superstructure, 137
  templates, 128–29
Textuality, 15, 69–70, 156n. 59
Texture, 102–3
Theoretical particularism, 11
Think-aloud-protocol, 30, 51
Toury, G., 8, 30, 32, 149n. 3
Translatability, 147
Translation
  bottom-up, 23
  competence, 37, 43
  computer-assisted, 27
  criticism, 17
  descriptive, 8
  evolution, 124
  expert systems for, 29
  heuristic, 31, 34, 53
  as interaction, 40
  as interdiscipline, 149n. 3
  machine, 27
  models of, 12
  —applied, 20, 22
  —computational, 26–29
  —critical, 16–18
  —first-order, 19, 33, 35
  —linguistic, 9, 10, 19–22, 44
  —practical, 18–19
  —psycholinguistic, 29–32

www.ingramcontent.com/pod-product-compliance
Lightning Source LLC
Chambersburg PA
CBHW022103160426
43198CB00008B/336